For Caroline and Alex

You are fearfully and wonderfully made. You have been searched and known before you were even born. If you take the wings of the morning and settle at the farthest limits of the sea, you are not alone. Even in your darkest nights, the light will be as bright as the day. (Inspired by Psalm 139)

PRAISE FOR
The Complete Business Leader

"I must thank Chris for sharing his knowledge on the key characteristics of the Complete Business Leader. Reading the book has illuminated the rationale for many of the steps that we innately take as leaders, engendering global best practice on the journey to deliver real results at the frontlines of development—in business and as non-state actors—as a practical framework for taking impact to scale. As we work together to ensure that primary health is the bedrock of the much-targeted Universal Health Coverage in my home country of Nigeria and around the world, I see *The Complete Business Leader* as a much-needed blueprint for future generations."

—HER EXCELLENCY TOYIN OJORA SARAKI,

Founder and President, Wellbeing Foundation Africa, Global Goodwill Ambassador, International Confederation of Midwives, Special Adviser to the Independent Advisory Group of the World Health Organization Regional Office for Africa

"Chris offers unique, actionable insights from three decades of experience during his rapid ascendancy from an individual contributor through the ranks of a junior manager to a CEO, building highly functioning teams at every stage. Readers will learn the benefits of an authentic style and keen sense of listening, learning, and understanding what it takes to achieve seemingly impossible goals."

—DONALD A. HOLZWORTH,

Global Health Entrepreneur, Founder, Constella Group, Executive in Residence at University of North Carolina, Gillings School of Global Public Health

"I first came to know Chris serving on the board of Futures Group where he was the CEO. I witnessed firsthand Chris's own journey through the leadership framework he presents. His authenticity, self-awareness, strategic perspective, and blend of business expertise and passion for making a contribution to global health all resonate for me in this book. *The Complete Business Leader* framework Chris lays out offers a vital roadmap for social enterprises of the future in helping us all achieve the sustainable development goals."

—AMBASSADOR MARK DYBUL, MD,

Co-Director, Center for Global Health Practice and Impact, Georgetown University Medical Center, former Executive Director, the Global Fund to Fight AIDS, Tuberculosis and Malaria, former US Global AIDS Coordinator

"Chris is among the savviest innovative leaders in our industry. Chris is a statistician by training, which means he uses hard facts as the basis for action that is deeply ingrained in his management decision-making. He has some unusually candid and compelling insights on the framework for a complete business leader . . . A must-read for young managers faced with making high-stakes decisions under increased pressure and uncertainty while managing personnel who are trying to find their way as well. Chris's reflections are practical, well meaning, and a much-needed contribution to our understanding of significant impactful management in the twenty-first century."

—ALONZO FULGHAM,

Career Member of the Senior Foreign Service, former Acting Administrator and Chief Operating Officer, US Agency for International Development

"Chris's generosity—sharing his thoughts, experiences, reflections—is part and parcel of how he shows up every day as a leader, colleague, and friend. It's great to see this now available to a wider audience as a tool for growth and success. The CBL model he's created indeed transcends borders, across countries, cultures, and sectors. I've seen his approaches transform projects, companies, and—most important—people, empowering them to best achieve their mission."

—SHANNON HADER, MD MPH,

Assistant Secretary General, United Nations Deputy Executive Director of Programme, UNAIDS

"In *The Complete Business Leader*, Chris comprehensively lays out the keys to success for professional services consulting firms by openly discussing both his successes and failures over the course of a thirty-year career. His folksy portrayal of his mentors and colleagues, complemented by literary and historical references, effectively illustrates the components of his user-friendly leadership development framework. The humble and insightful commentary about his own personal journey is both refreshing and impactful. This is a must-read for those who are striving throughout their careers for expanded awareness and leadership skills development that enhances personal and organizational satisfaction and success."

—E. WAYNE HOLDEN, PHD,

President and Chief Executive Officer, RTI International, Adjunct Professor, Department of Psychiatry and Behavioral Sciences, Duke University School of Medicine, Adjunct Professor, The Gillings School of Global Public Health, University of North Carolina at Chapel Hill

THE COMPLETE BUSINESS LEADER

A Framework for Impact in Work and Life

CHRISTOPHER A. LEGRAND

Contents

Preface..xiii

Chris LeGrand's Winding Career Journey xvii

Chapter 1. Introduction to the Complete Business
Leader...1
Some Definitional Thinking 1
The Complete Business Leader Framework...................... 3
Evolution of the Framework.............................. 5
How the Book Is Structured 10

Chapter 2. Individual Wisdom 13
Competencies of Individual Wisdom 15
    Curiosity..15
    Continuous learning..17
    Self-confidence 19
    Courageous.. 20
    Cool under pressure 24
    Independently responsible 26
    Organized... 30
    Generous 32
Summary Comments... 34

Chapter 3. Relationship Management 37
Competencies of Relationship Management.................... 40
    Institutional representation 41
    Taking the long view 42
    Creating common ground 45

Mutual respect 46
Engagement.. 49
Responsiveness 51
Standing for the other 53
Summary Comments.. 55

Chapter 4. Thought Leadership **59**
Competencies of Thought Leadership 62
Active externally 63
Innovator... 67
Active internally... 73
Summary Comments 77

Chapter 5. Business Growth **81**
Competencies of Business Growth 89
Opportunity development 89
Capture management...................................... 93
Proposal development 98
Strategic Business Growth Through M&A.......... 104
Summary Comments.. 106

Chapter 6. People Leadership **109**
Competencies of People Leadership 112
Selection 112
Development 115
Delegation.. 120
Example.. 125
Summary Comments.. 129

Chapter 7. Project Management **131**
Competencies of Project Management 134
Organized... 134

Disciplined 139
Analytical 144
Communication 148
Summary Comments 151

Chapter 8. Business Management 155
Competencies of Business Management 159
Governance and legal awareness 159
Risk management 164
Financial acumen 167
Strategic perspective 173
Summary Comments 178

Chapter 9. Complete Business Leader in Action 181
CBL Program Implementation 185
CBL Program Evaluation 189
CBL Program Impact 191

Chapter 10. Concluding Thoughts 197

Appendix 1: CBL Competencies 207

Appendix 2: Resources and Tools 217

Appendix 3: Real Leaders Referenced in the Book 221

Notes 225

Bibliography 229

About the Authors 231

ACKNOWLEDGMENTS

I have many acknowledgments to make. In my career journey, there are so many who have had an impact on me or informed my thinking that it is virtually impossible to capture them all. But here I'll acknowledge a few who had the most impact on the development of the Complete Business Leader model.

My first boss, Frank O'Brien (rest in peace, 2011), a great mentor and friend who modeled unpretentious, selfless leadership for me; David Walker, a brilliant CFO and early boss who believed in me more than I believed in myself and gave me an on-the-job MBA; John Cook, former boss and longtime mentor and friend who showed me the value of personal relationships; Don Holzworth, who saw greatness in me and from whom I learned too much to catalogue in the thirteen years we worked together; several longtime business colleagues and friends, including Susan Acker-Walsh, Linda Holt, and Kathleen Schindler (rest in peace, 2017), who challenged me, called out my blind spots, and took stands for me to be my best self as a leader; and Jane Smith, my executive coach for twelve years, who was my champion and my accountability partner.

I also want to thank and acknowledge Liz Mallas, a friend and colleague who fully embraced and began to practice the Complete Business Leader framework, studied and tested the framework as part of a master's degree program, and authored in its entirety Chapter 9 of this book.

I thank my twenty-four-year-old, all-grown-up daughter, Caroline, a fabulous writer herself, who did a first deep edit for me on the manuscript and made the book better. My work on her is done. Now she is working on me.

Most important, I thank Susan, my wife and love of twenty-nine years now, who embodies selfless service to others and walked away from a rising career in banking to be at home for our children and manage our household. She has stood by me and for me, put up with my moods and my mild OCD, and kept the fires burning while I commuted to DC and traveled the world.

PREFACE

In launching into this endeavor of writing a book, in justifying my time and energy to write this, I have thought to myself, why do we need yet another book on management and leadership? And maybe that is true. So I had to answer that for myself first. And I have had to answer for myself questions like, Do I have anything useful, new, and compelling to say? Why should anybody care? Will this be different and contradictory to well-known and respected management and leadership pundits? Have I earned enough respect or clout, even if I do have something useful to say, to be taken seriously?

The fact that I am writing the book and you are reading it means I have answered those questions to my satisfaction and hopefully will answer them to yours. The fact that I had to convince myself first should give you some comfort that what you will read here is of value. Because I know that my time is valuable. And your time is valuable. I know that in a world of 280-character tweets, Instagram likes, and "endorsements" on LinkedIn, for anyone to read a whole book, it needs to add value. You have a right to expect value from this book. In short, I wrote this book and I think you should read it because I have something to say that I believe has value. The book should speak to you whether you are a twenty-three-year-old starting a career, a mid-career mid-level leader, an entrepreneur, or a senior executive in a large business. And whether your organization is that large business, a small business, a nonprofit, or even a church, you should find some nuggets of value to mine.

Let me say at the outset, though, that this is not a how-to book. The value derived here is not from learning a cookbook guide of new skills to practice to become a better leader. This is a concepts book. And those who know me will tell you that is consistent with who I am—I am a macro to micro thinker, a person who conceives and structures thought and life from context and conceptual frameworks first before moving to tactical practices and skills. That is not to say that practices and skill development are not valuable; in fact, ultimately practices that turn into everyday actions are where life and leadership happen. But I just wanted to set the expectation that where I start is at the conceptual.

So this is a book about a leadership framework: the Complete Business Leader. This framework didn't come out of a classroom or academic setting at one of the great MBA schools, though I have deep respect for the thinking there. This framework didn't come from a CEO who has run a Fortune 100 public company, like Jack Welch, though I have admired his management and leadership thinking for many years. This framework didn't come from a TED-talking leadership consultant, though I have heard and experienced these and taken valuable insights from them. Though individual elements of the Complete

Business Leader (CBL) could be attributed to other experts in leadership and have been informed by many of my colleagues and fellow leaders, the framework as a whole package is my creation, my way of thinking about and ordering leadership.

I am an aging guy with normal insecurities, triumphs, and trials, but by most people's accounts I would be deemed a successful business leader, having risen over my thirty-two-year career from a junior statistician to the CEO of a global company. So the Complete Business Leader framework presented in this book is conceptual but based on real-world business leadership experience from someone who grew and learned through a range of companies and roles; in that sense, it is practical and hands on.

The framework is also real in that it has already been in use for organizing people and leadership development in two prior companies I have been involved with. And it has evolved over time as I have learned, observed, and experimented in various leadership settings. The framework and this book are the culmination of my experiences, my study and learning, my coaches and mentors, and my failures and successes along that thirty-plus-year journey.

As you read, you might also recognize aspects of other leaders you have encountered or aspects of yourself somewhere in the book if you have been out in the world professionally. And that's a great thing, as none of us has cornered the market on good ideas and great leadership.

One thing imprinted in me from early on by my parents, particularly my mom, was determination. When I was sick (as I was frequently as a young child), or tired, or knocked down, I learned from my mom's steely determination to just get up and keep going and engage in the world. My mom would just look at me and say, "Take two Tylenol and go on." So that's what I've done—my whole career and my whole life. Never stopping until something is complete. This book is, at its core, a product of that determination.

I hope you enjoy reading *The Complete Business Leader.*

Take two Tylenol and go on . . .

—**Clista H. LeGrand**

Chris LeGrand's Winding Career Journey

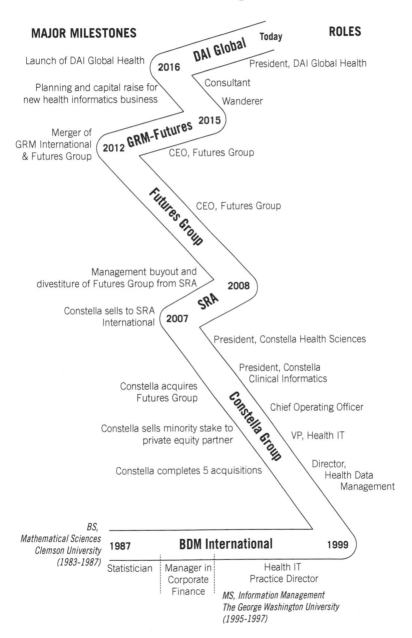

MAJOR MILESTONES

ROLES

Launch of DAI Global Health

DAI Global

Today

President, DAI Global Health

2016

Consultant

Planning and capital raise for new health informatics business

Wanderer

2015

Merger of GRM International & Futures Group

2012 GRM-Futures

CEO, Futures Group

Futures Group

CEO, Futures Group

Management buyout and divestiture of Futures Group from SRA

2008

SRA

Constella sells to SRA International

2007

President, Constella Health Sciences

President, Constella Clinical Informatics

Constella acquires Futures Group

Constella Group

Chief Operating Officer

Constella sells minority stake to private equity partner

VP, Health IT

Constella completes 5 acquisitions

Director, Health Data Management

BS, Mathematical Sciences Clemson University (1983-1987)

1987

BDM International

1999

Statistician | Manager in Corporate Finance | Health IT Practice Director

MS, Information Management The George Washington University (1995-1997)

INTRODUCTION TO THE COMPLETE BUSINESS LEADER

The problem with the title of this leadership framework is the word "complete." It implies that there is a point at which you've arrived or will arrive, that there is a point—a measurable point—at which you are complete. But this book, this framework, is actually about a pilgrimage, not a destination. On a pilgrimage there may be a series of stops, but it is really about the trials, learning, and growth that you experience along the way. It is what you learn about yourself and who you are becoming as you walk the road. So this book is not about arriving as a Complete Business Leader. It is about the journey *toward becoming* a Complete Business Leader—a journey that is never completed.

SOME DEFINITIONAL THINKING

With that, let me start with my basic premise: *Organizations of any size and focus will have bigger impact and be more successful by any measure when their leaders are well rounded and grounded, can integrate across disciplines, and can inspire diverse followers to produce results.* Organizations need Complete Business Leaders. Complete Business Leaders have mastered a series of **dimensions** needed to be successful in work and life. And here is the paradox: Complete Business Leaders realize their incompleteness. As soon as a leader believes they have arrived, that immediately confirms they have not.

Here are a few other simple principles on which this leadership framework is based. Though these are generally accepted in business parlance, I want to highlight them for clarity:

- o Management is not the same as leadership.
- o A "leader" is not restricted to an executive who manages a group or function. A leader can be an individual contributor.
- o You can actually be a manager and not be a leader (you just won't be an *effective* manager).

Another important premise of mine is that you can grow and transform yourself as a leader no matter where you are on the leadership journey. Some believe that you are born as a leader or that your basic traits are honed and don't really change after about age twenty-five. I believe whether or not someone is born with certain traits, individuals can develop themselves throughout their lives if they are truly committed to that. This book and this framework presumes you can continue to develop yourself as an increasingly Complete Business Leader throughout your career.

And a few words about why the word "business" is in the title of the framework. Some might say, "Well, this doesn't apply to me because I work for a nonprofit or a faith-based organization." Early on, I thought about dropping that word from the name of the framework. Yet I believe that many of the leadership competencies described in the book apply to those in organizational constructs beyond only for-profit companies.

Reexamining the etymology of the word, before the word came to be synonymous with commerce, I think the word "business" totally captures what I mean as a complete *business* leader. Older definitions back to Middle English include "care, anxiety, occupation" or "the state of being occupied or engaged" or "that which is taken on as a duty" or "a person's work."[1] All of these apply to a person trying to create something of value for the world, whether that's giving a helping hand to the marginalized via a nonprofit organization, feeding the hungry and saving souls in a faith-based organization, or creating products and services in a for-profit company.

THE COMPLETE BUSINESS LEADER FRAMEWORK

The Complete Business Leader (CBL) framework consists of seven dimensions. See the chart below. Each dimension has a set of competencies—or skills—that can be developed. Some might call these "disciplines." Each competency has a set of behaviors or characteristics, the outward display of which is an indication of the competency. I have structured this framework as distinct dimensions, competencies, and behaviors, but in many cases there are tight connections and interdependencies among these. The seven dimensions do not necessarily have a hierarchy except that the first dimension, *Individual Wisdom,* is foundational to all other dimensions. If you are of a Judeo-Christian faith background, you might think of this as analogous to Jesus saying that the first two commandments are more important than all others because they set the stage for all the others.

Organizational Ethos		
People Leadership	Project Management	Business Management
Business Growth		
Thought Leadership		
Relationship Management		
Individual Wisdom		

It is important to note that the CBL framework comes to life within the specific context of a particular organization—its mission, values, industry, and business model. I am calling this context the "organizational ethos." The way I am using it, ethos is the distinguishing character (from the first part of Merriam-Webster's definition) of the organization—the combination of attributes that, taken together, make the organization clearly recognizable from the inside and outside.

This is similar to Jim Collins's definition of "core ideology" in his landmark book *Built to Last.* These contextual factors influence significantly which aspects of leadership work and don't work. In other words, the specific dimensions of the framework and associated competencies play out differently in different organizations.

For example, I once had a senior leader who had been very successful in a government bureaucracy in a developing country. This person was highly regarded, revered almost, inside this particular government. When this person came into my company's context, however, she struggled. Her leadership persona did not work in our environment. Almost every aspect of how she had led successfully in her government executive role ended up being unworkable in her senior leadership role in our company. So while at a high level the elements of being a Complete Business Leader are universal, the specific instantiations (behaviors and habits) may need to look somewhat different in different organizations.

EVOLUTION OF THE FRAMEWORK

So where did this framework come from? It's from my own career journey with its own highs and lows, experiences and learnings. The chart just before this Introduction chapter depicts graphically my winding career journey and the companies I have been involved with, which may be helpful as an occasional reference guide throughout the book.

I started documenting the CBL framework around 2005 and continued to tweak and evolve it based on new learnings and experiences. At a previous company, Constella Group, where I served in expanding leadership capacities eventually to run a large portion of the business as president of its public sector business, I began to move the framework from a notional theory in my head to a practical, detailed framework for hiring and developing leaders. When I later became CEO of Futures Group, a global professional services business, I continued evolving the framework and put it into practice in how we hired, developed, and evaluated leaders. So at both Constella and Futures Group, the Complete Business Leader framework came to life in a real-world organizational context to hire, evaluate, and develop leaders.

When I started my career in the late 1980s at BDM International, which at the time was the preeminent government professional services company, I was told early on about a concept referred to as the "triple threat." A triple threat was someone who could win business, manage projects, and manage people. At BDM, the few who were considered triple threats were specially groomed and given substantial responsibilities and opportunities.

I was fortunate enough to be seen early in my career as a triple threat. Early on at BDM I found I had a proficiency in managing projects and a natural nose for sniffing out and securing new business. And fairly quickly I was able to use my leadership experiences and people skills that I gained from university in beginning to supervise people. The triple threat notion captures three of the seven CBL dimensions: *Project Management, People Leadership, and Business Growth*.

After a few years, though, I recognized that there was a missing link for me. I didn't understand how my work related to BDM's overall financial and business success. So I took a career risk and BDM took that risk with me, moving me out of the line revenue-generating side of the company to a role in corporate finance, a staff function.

In my three years in corporate finance, I learned more on the job than most MBA programs could teach. I learned from a brilliant CFO. I learned the inextricable links between individual projects and how they rolled up to the corporate financial picture. I learned why certain decisions I had made as a project manager might be bad decisions from a corporate perspective and vice versa. I learned why getting client invoices out the door and getting paid quickly was important to cash flow. I learned about the factors that optimized both projects and the organization as a whole. This experience is where I began to learn a fourth dimension of the CBL: *Business Management*.

After three years in corporate finance, I had a choice to make. By then I was running a small finance team (*People Leadership*), and my boss was clearly grooming me for a career path in corporate finance. Realizing I was narrowing my future career prospects, I asked to get off the finance path and back into the revenue-producing side of the business. I was in the fortunate position through having built strong relationships with the various executive leaders of BDM such that when I asked to move back to the revenue side of the business, a path was made for me.

So after three years in corporate finance, I walked away from the clear career path in finance back into the murky world of professional services at BDM. I was assigned to a group doing medical systems modeling and analysis. I brought with me an advanced understanding of the overall business but was now three years behind my peers in technical expertise (the product we were selling).

Back in the role of managing projects and people and now managing a set of client relationships, I felt ill prepared. I was not an expert in what I was selling and delivering.

I had to rely on others when it came to more technical matters. While this might work in some organizational contexts, at BDM I had a hard time gaining the respect of my staff, my boss, my peers, and my clients. BDM was a very technically driven organization; it valued technical prowess above most other things.

I struggled to gain my footing for several years, even flirting once with being fired. My immediate supervisor at that point clearly didn't respect me technically and didn't see value in the corporate financial acumen I brought, so she tried to drive me out of the organization. She undermined me with my team, our client, and executive management. It was a painful couple of years.

It was then that I decided to pursue a master's degree in systems engineering and information technology management at night while I worked full time. I realized I needed to become a technical expert, a thought leader, in a technical area. I wrote position papers and started taking on technical parts of projects; after a while I developed an unassailable technical expertise. In fact, the subject of my master's thesis in 1997 was the privacy of health information in the internet age, a harbinger of what would become a major philosophical, political, and policy issue over the past twenty years. My thesis focused specifically on what, at the time, was the newly passed Health Insurance Portability and Accountability Act (HIPAA). I had become a technical expert on health information privacy. And here is where I learned a fifth element of the CBL: *Thought Leadership.*

After recovering my footing at BDM and finishing strong, running a portfolio of health IT programs and clients, I left the company, we moved to a new state, and I took a role with a small business in North Carolina, Constella Group.

From 1999 to 2007, I grew and Constella grew. I started out at Constella managing a thirty-five-person team and by 2007 was leading a 1000+ person global business unit working in thirty-five countries. Along that part of the journey, I honed and put into practice much of what is now presented in the CBL framework. I watched and learned relationship management from the founder of Constella, Don Holzworth. Don had complete mastery of relationships—staff, clients, partners, bankers, investors, politicians, board members, and the general business community. This is where I learned a sixth element of the CBL: *Relationship Management.*

Along my entire career pilgrimage, I have been learning about the foundational CBL dimension: *Individual Wisdom*. I learned most and saw how it impacts my effectiveness as a leader at Constella Group and then later as CEO of Futures Group.

Individual Wisdom is foundational to and integrated into all other parts of the CBL framework. Each of the other CBL dimensions can be mastered only in the face of increasing mastery individual wisdom. In this area, I attribute my own development in large part to Jane Smith of Dorrier Underwood Consulting, who was my executive coach for twelve years. Being on the path to self-awareness enables me to be increasingly complete in all other dimensions of the CBL. Being progressively more wise about who I am, how I occur and want to occur in the world, what I am good at and not good at, and what I want people and the world left with as a result of me having spent time on the earth gave me the courage to walk away from Futures Group and start something new.

I engineered the successful merger of Futures Group, stayed for three years to ensure a smooth transition, and moved into the next phase of my own career and life pilgrimage. That next phase involved being out on my own, intentionally wandering around in the wilderness (considerably longer than forty days), a bit hungry and thirsty some days for the fulfillment of running a large organization that makes money and makes a positive impact on the world.

On my own, I started building out and pitching a new business idea to investors: the idea of creating a global health informatics business that would harness the power of information to help people around the globe live healthier lives. The idea involved acquiring multiple small niche businesses and combining them onto one informatics platform. In parallel, I did some strategic consulting engagements for friends and colleagues in other large organizations. Without an organizational anchor, I also used that time to soul-search and deepen my individual wisdom. And to start writing this book along the way.

Toward the end of that year in the wilderness, one of the friends I was doing some consulting for, the CEO of a highly respected company named DAI, proposed that I build out my new business idea but do it as part of DAI. After a couple of months of "no thank yous," I became convinced that I could build out my new business idea, and the next phase of my career, at DAI. So, at the start of 2016, I joined DAI to launch a global health business.

HOW THE BOOK IS STRUCTURED

I devote a chapter of the book to each of these seven dimensions, describing in detail the specific competencies of each dimension and specific outward behaviors or characteristics that demonstrate the competencies. I then illuminate those behaviors and competencies with specific stories of how I have seen them modeled well or poorly by leaders I have encountered or studied.

Later in the book I also devote a chapter (Chapter 9) to a real-world description of how the Complete Business Leader framework was tested as part of a structured organizational design study in a real-world company setting. This study involved a selected cohort of leaders who went through a twelve-month leadership intensive program geared specifically around the Complete Business Leader framework. The leaders in the cohort all went through several industry standard benchmark evaluative instruments at the beginning of the program to establish a baseline and were evaluated again at the end of the twelve-month program. So this cohort program provides a good lab experiment on developing more Complete Business Leaders via the framework laid out in this book.

This evaluation chapter, called "Complete Business Leader in Action," is authored by Elizabeth (Liz) Mallas, a business colleague and friend. Liz, at midcareer, is already far down the path of becoming a Complete Business Leader herself. She was intrigued by the CBL model and offered to lead an endeavor at Palladium (the merged company of Futures Group and GRM International) to develop the cohort program. She designed and then coordinated the program, which included selecting the leadership evaluation instruments from best practice in the people development / organizational development community.

The book contains three appendices. In Appendix 1, you'll find a set of tables delineating the key competencies and specific characteristics of each CBL dimension. These tables are found also at the end of their respective chapters but are combined into one appendix for ease of reference. Appendix 2 contains a catalogue of tools, aids, and other readings I have found helpful and influential in the implementation and continuing evolution of the CBL. Appendix 3 contains a summary table of various leaders I refer to in the book who likely are not household names, but I owe them reference, as they are some of the many from whom I have learned much. After the appendices, you'll find endnotes and a bibliography and at the end of the book you'll find short biographical sketches of Liz Mallas and me under About the Authors.

The examples I use of leaders at their best and worst hopefully bring the framework to life for you. These stories come from politics, military, art, sports, and business—real and imagined leaders. In positive leadership examples, I have referenced names; in negative cases (counterexamples), I have generally left their names out. The examples from my own experience in business are all real, not imagined, and to the best of my memory happened in the way I describe them. When I use examples of political leaders, I am expressly *not* making a political statement; rather, I am looking through a leadership lens.

Since I am not yet a Complete Business Leader, I welcome your feedback and leadership examples from your own experience that map to elements of the CBL framework. Please reach out to me. My contact information can be found at www.thecompletebusinessleader.com. So let's dissect what it looks like to be a Complete Business Leader.

INDIVIDUAL WISDOM

"I wish it need not have happened in my time," said Frodo.
"So do I," said Gandalf, "and so do all who live to see such times. But that is not for them to
decide. All we have to decide is what to do with the time that is given us."
—J. R. R. Tolkien, *The Fellowship of the Ring*

Gandalf got me through high school. As I was coming of age, experiencing the trials that some do in high school, the old wizard from J. R. R. Tolkien's *The Hobbit* and The Lord of the Rings was there for me. Gandalf's warm, knowing eyes, boisterous laugh, fierce loyalty, penetrating questions, ability to read people or a situation and the context around him, and instinctual feel for what to do next—these all gave me the courage to move forward in dark times. I read *The Hobbit* and then The Lord of the Rings books for the first time when I was in a deep depression in high school. Since then, I have reread these books in succession three additional times. Gandalf embodies "individual wisdom" as I am defining it. From time to time in the rest of this chapter on *Individual Wisdom*, I'll refer back to Gandalf. If you don't know his character, I encourage to you to explore it as a model for *Individual Wisdom*.

Individual Wisdom is at the core of the CBL framework, meaning that a leader cannot master the other six dimensions of the CBL framework without mastering himself or herself first. When I describe some specific competencies of *Individual Wisdom* below, this premise will become more self-evident.

As I noted earlier, I have been on my own pilgrimage toward *Individual Wisdom*. A critical part of that journey was my twelve-year relationship with an executive coach. During that time I also participated in several leadership intensive workshops and courses, the essence of which was getting clarity about who I am and am not, what I am choosing to stand for as a leader, how I occur and want to occur in the world—in short, being increasingly self-aware and actualized.

While someone could conceivably develop this self-awareness alone in a monastery, having a coach and going through leadership intensives is, in my experience, an accelerant. Coaches, if they are good, are like a mirror for you. They help you see yourself and how you occur in the world. Coaches, if they are good, call you out when others won't or can't. Coaches, if they are good, cut through all of the outer clothing we sometimes adorn ourselves with and help us discover and develop our essence as effective human beings. This is not about the strategies and tactics of business and management, though consultants of that ilk are valuable. This is about the strategies and tactics of leadership and life.

Before we jump into these competencies, let me just say clearly now that being wise and increasingly self-aware does not mean being perfect. Someone who is wise is certainly still going take a wrong turn, make a bad decision, or sometimes misjudge a situation. But that wise leader will quickly see their misstep and recover and will also be self-aware enough to be responsible for their own flaw in the situation.

Below I'll highlight key competencies of *Individual Wisdom*. For each competency, I describe it in detail, give some real leadership examples plus some examples of NOT exhibiting that competency, and share vignettes of how the competency plays out in the real world. I should note here that I while I am describing these competencies linearly for simplicity, the reality is that they are interconnected and somewhat overlapping in both learning and application. From time to time, I'll also use an example from my favorite wizard, Gandalf.

COMPETENCIES OF INDIVIDUAL WISDOM

CURIOSITY. The first key competency of *Individual Wisdom* is curiosity. Being curious comes from a humble place of knowing you don't know things and wanting to know them. Or even if you think you know, exhibiting a willingness to challenge what you think you know. Even if they know a lot, curious people yearn to know more. They ask lots of questions of others, as well as frequently stepping back and questioning their own knowledge, assumptions, biases, and motivations.

Gandalf was curious. He would sit back, puff on his pipe, with his big bushy eyebrows furrowed as he asked questions of himself and others. No matter that he had lived for many hundreds of years and could, then, be assumed to have encountered just about everything in life.

Curiosity includes asking, "What do I not know?" or "What does this person think?" and may also include "Why do I not know?" or "Why does this person think this?" One of the business colleagues I revere and remember most was the human resources senior executive at Constella Group, Rich Podurgal. In addition to being able to connect the dots from the HR world to the broader business context, which many times HR folks are not geared to do, he embodied curiosity. He asked questions, sought to understand, listened intently, and drove conversations deeper than the superficial answers that might be given at first. Even if he thought he understood or knew the answer, he modeled authentic curiosity by digging deeper to help himself and others make better decisions and run the company more effectively.

Sometimes his inquisitiveness drove me crazy—I just wanted him to give me his opinion and recommendation—but I grew to appreciate his approach. He and I struck a great business partnership, and I learned a great deal from him. The antithesis of this would be, say, a politician who takes a bold stand on an issue and drives a policy or action without the curiosity of asking questions like "What are the real facts and data?" "Who is giving me information and what are their motives?" "What are the possible unintended consequences?" or "What am I missing?"

Curiosity may come more naturally for some than others, but you can practice being curious, like any other behavior, by teaching yourself to ask the questions and learning to regularly interrogate your own knowledge.

Of course, curiosity and inquisitiveness must be balanced by bold, decisive action when called for. There are situations where great leaders have to act now and ask questions later. So I am not saying that complete leaders should get bogged down in curiosity, endlessly questioning themselves or others. Rather, individually wise leaders know both when to question and when to act. Even when they have moved to action, individually wise leaders continue to be curious, evaluating the decisions they have made.

Balancing these seemingly conflicting leadership competencies—curiosity and action—is part of the leadership challenge. But as a general rule of thumb, great leaders exhibit a curiousness. This causes them to seek out new ideas, find new problems to solve, and incorporate new knowledge. A leader can never know all the information, but choosing curiosity as a leadership way of "being" generates wiser leaders and wiser decisions.

CONTINUOUS LEARNING. Another key competency of *Individual Wisdom* is continuous learning (see Chapter 4, *Thought Leadership*, where this concept is also discussed). Regardless of the field of study where someone is considered a thought leader, there are new ideas, concepts, and knowledge being developed constantly. To remain a thought leader in that field, the leader must have a thirst for continuing to learn. The leader must take the view that they have never learned all they can about the subject, even if they are considered one of the world's experts in that area.

One of my longtime business colleagues, Farley Cleghorn, is considered a world-renowned expert in HIV/AIDS. Yet he carves out at least a portion of every day to read and study the latest published research or meet with others in the field to learn and share. He also contributes to the professional body of knowledge.

And back to The Lord of the Rings: When Gandalf wasn't sure about the origins of Bilbo's magic ring and had only a vague sense of its possible terrible connection to the past, he took off to an old library and immersed himself in research and study. He poured over ancient texts, compared notes with others, and displayed the urgency and intensity required to discover and learn. Also, Gandalf learned from his own mistakes. He was initially fooled by Saruman, his old wizard mentor. Gandalf missed the signs that Saruman had turned evil because he was blinded by his loyalty and respect. But once Saruman revealed his true intent and attempted to convince Gandalf to join him, Gandalf wasn't fooled by him again.

When I moved to North Carolina and went to work for Constella Group, one of the rewarding and energizing things about the business culture was a state of continuous learning. At Constella, I found an environment that craved new ideas and ways of doing things—one that was eager to try new things. Many times when seasoned leaders come into a new organization and try to bring new ideas, they are met with a wave of passive or active resistance, the "that's not how we do it here" phenomenon. Not at Constella. What I found when I arrived there was a welcoming culture that said, "You're the new guy. Now show us some new ways to do things."

A more recent example is my short time with the combined GRM–Futures Group (now branded Palladium). Though I stayed around for only three years after closing the merger of Futures Group with GRM International, I appreciated the culture of continuous learning that GRM's senior executives exhibited. Though they controlled the merger, their senior most leaders didn't presume they had all the answers. They sought out new ways to do things and were totally open to learning new approaches from their junior merger partner, my Futures Group team and me. In fact, GRM senior leaders eagerly sought out new learnings on corporate operations, human resources, leadership development, and so forth.

SELF-CONFIDENCE. Another competency of *Individual Wisdom* is self-confidence. Barnes & Noble currently lists 705 book titles on the subject of self-confidence, so I will not try to recreate all the how-tos of those books. I'll just describe my own experience of it. Self-confidence comes not just from experience and knowledge but from knowing: knowing what you know, knowing what you don't know, and knowing who you are and who you are not. That knowing from within oneself gets projected externally as self-confidence. In my experience, followers gravitate to self-confident leaders, which is why this competency is so critical.

Here is a personal example. I am self-confident and convey that in the area of pursuing and winning new large government contracts, including the intense thirty to forty-five days associated with preparing the competitive proposal for a government contract. Though I don't get deeply involved in these efforts much anymore, when I do, my way of being is clear and comforting to others around me. I am self-confident because I have been through it many times before (experience), have a demonstrated track record of success, and know what I know and don't know.

During the heat of the proposal period, things almost always get chaotic, tempers get short, and people worry. I can dive into the capture or proposal process at any point on almost any project and convey that self-confidence, which gets people refocused on the task at hand. I also have nothing left to prove in this particular area and can just be helpful.

One way self-confidence manifests itself is in a leader being willing to be vulnerable. This doesn't mean constant self-deprecation or falling on one's sword all the time—I think this gets tiresome coming from a leader. But it does mean a leader is comfortable enough to say, "My fault," or "I screwed up," without worrying about losing followers. One of the markers I have used in the past several years to evaluate leaders who work for or with me is listening for them to say the phrase "I screwed up." If I never hear that from a leader, then they don't advance in my team because it means they are not self-aware or confident enough to see where they messed up and call themselves out on it.

Now, there is a fine line between self-confidence and arrogance. Some followers like what we might call cockiness in a leader, but to others it is a turnoff. The wise, complete leader is able to walk that fine line and convey what is needed, when needed, for the followers who need it. Discovering how to walk that fine line may work differently for different leaders, but I have found that my spouse and children are the best benchmarks for me on the self-confidence to arrogance continuum. They will ALWAYS let me know when I have moved over into arrogance!

COURAGEOUS. Wise leaders display a competency of being courageous. This means making hard decisions, having hard conversations, and taking on hard tasks. It means taking on something or someone you don't want to take on, getting up when you are beaten down, and being willing to deal with whatever consequences may come from a decision.

Courage sometimes means just picking a path and starting down it, even when the way is totally unclear and you really have no idea whether it's the best path or not. Courage means charting a course, taking something on, when the hoped for outcome is far from certain. One of my favorite examples of courage was the bold choice to go to the moon. President Kennedy, in his famous speech at Rice University in 1962, declared not only that the United States would send a man to the moon and back but would do so within the decade. Of course he didn't live to see it, but his courageous leadership proclamation inspired action and followers.

> We choose to go to the moon in this decade, and do the other things,
> not because they are easy but because they are hard . . .
> **—President John F. Kennedy, 1962**

Courageous leaders take on hard things, sometimes just because they are hard. What Kennedy went on to say in that speech at Rice was that taking on hard things brings out the best in people: "That goal will serve to organize and measure the best of our energies and skills . . ."

Many years ago, my boss and founder of Constella Group, Don Holzworth, took on having our organization pursue a large contract that would more than double the size of the company if we won. It would transform our organization so as to be almost unrecognizable from what it was before. Don faced many skeptics among his own leadership team and certainly externally. If we failed, we would have been diminished in the industry and would have spent a major portion of the company's free cash flow pursuing it.

He took that on and called on his whole team to be great and achieve more than they ever imagined (see also Chapter 6, *People Leadership*) precisely because he knew it was hard. He knew that goal would organize and measure the best. And of course, we did win. And it did transform our company. And in it is a lesson in *Individual Wisdom*.

It takes courage to have a hard conversation with a colleague, a client, someone who works for you, a boss, or a board member. This hard conversation might include admitting that you screwed up or telling someone else they screwed up. It might mean speaking out when something is not working or workable. A hard conversation has risk and likely has conflict. In spite of that risk and our human nature to avoid conflict (even some strong leaders tend to avoid conflict), wise leaders have hard conversations. One of the best resources I have seen on this component of *Individual Wisdom* is a book called *Fierce Conversations* by Susan Scott. There are training offerings based on the same material as well.

My executive coach, Jane Smith, helped me over the years to have numerous hard conversations with bosses, people who were my colleagues or worked for me, and even clients. Fifteen years ago I had a very difficult time having hard conversations. I would lose sleep, make caveats, equivocate, and procrastinate. But over the years I have practiced having hard conversations (many times). Sometimes I would just pick a hard conversation to have, even if it were not so critical.

With practice comes muscle. What I learned through that practice, and with help from my coach, was the technique of writing down what I was really committed to and how that related to the outcome from the conversation I wanted. This helped me get clear about why the conversation was important to have, even if it made me uncomfortable. The situation became about my level of commitment to overcome the difficulty of the conversation. I am generally considered a "nice" guy, and hard conversations are still not my favorite thing to do, but I am also now a leader who will not hesitate to have the hard conversation when needed.

The courageous business leader gets to the heart of the matter to solve problems. Another way of saying it is that the courageous leader seeks and finds the source of issues rather than dithering around the symptoms. Treating symptoms or corollary issues is usually easier and has less short-term risk, so many leaders stay at the symptoms level.

The pastor at my church in McLean, Virginia, exhibited this behavior of getting to the heart of the matter. He was empathetic and gracious yet had a knack for drilling deeply to core issues quickly, even when they were uncomfortable or risky. Once in the mid-1990s there was a traumatic issue for our church that had the potential to split the church in two. This issue was a powder keg with many tangentially related issues and complex emotional dynamics.

Rather than let this fester, let people talk behind peoples' backs and separate camps to form, he went right to the heart of the matter. He spoke to individuals one on one and in larger group settings. He took on the harder root issue rather than all of the secondary issues and red herrings bouncing around. By courageously modeling this, he also helped the members have the hard conversations we needed to have with each other. While a few members did leave over this potentially divisive issue, most stayed, we found a compromise and a way forward, and we all grew as a result.

Courage is *not* about being fearless. It is acting in spite of that fear. Gandalf had fear. In one place in the Tolkien story, Gandalf hears in his mind the words of his former mentor and now nemesis saying, "Moria, you fear to go into those mines. . . . You know what they awoke in the darkness . . ."

Gandalf is leading his small party on their quest and desperately wants to avoid going through the mines underneath the mountain. Yet eventually that proves to be the path that must be taken, so Gandalf courageously leads on. And before he has led his group safely to the other side, he does have to face down his worst fear of the fire monster deep in the bowels of the mountain. He faces that fear and stands against it to save his group, even to his own peril.

For leaders in the business world, this fear could be of fear of embarrassment or looking bad, losing a major investment, losing respect, getting fired, and so forth. Every business leader I know has experienced some of these kinds of inner fears, these "dark nights of the soul" (St. John of the Cross). Courageous business leaders push through these fears when they are committed to achieving something.

COOL UNDER PRESSURE. All leaders will eventually face adversity and unexpected challenges—that is, if they are causing anything of any consequence to happen. Individually wise leaders face that pressure with calm. They rally people to them with a demeanor, a way of occurring, that says, "We've got this."

Situations that are uncertain or ambiguous, or where the context is chaotic and dangerous, bring out the best in wise leaders. The wise leader provides clarity and a way forward in the face of that chaos when others can't or won't. Wise leaders thrive on it and seem to almost seek it out.

Gandalf exhibited this cool-under-pressure competency many times in Tolkien's story. The situation could be chaotic, the way forward would be murky, the other members of his band of adventurers would be lost and bickering among themselves, but Gandalf would calm and focus the group and get them moving forward. In one situation, Gandalf and a hobbit, Pippin, are barricaded inside the White City, which is under attack. They sit just inside a main city gate that is soon to be overrun with their enemies. Chaos abounds: people are running wildly everywhere, shouting and trying to flee; arrows are flying all around; and the enemy is pounding on the door with a battering ram about to break through. Their impending death is almost certain.

Pippin is terrified and frozen and says to Gandalf, "I didn't think it would end like this." Gandalf calmly comforts him, saying, "End? No, the journey doesn't end here. Death is just another path, one that we all must take." He then goes on to describe a beautiful, calm scene after death, to which Pippin says, "Well, that isn't so bad." Gandalf's words and his way of being bring calm and focus for Pippin, allowing Pippin move into action when the city wall is finally breached. He fights with abandon, confident now that death is just another path and "isn't so bad."

As a real-world example, I'll highlight a situation at BDM from early in my career. I was in a fifty-person work group that had one large contract upon which all of our jobs depended. That contract was up for rebid; right in the middle of the rebidding proposal process, the head of our work group had a heart attack and was out of commission. Suddenly we were leaderless. The proposal process, as was typical of government contracts proposals, was already chaotic, intense, and nerve-wracking for all of our group. We knew if we lost that proposal, we were all out of jobs.

Now our leader was gone. He was the one we all trusted and assumed would lead us to victory. I remember the sheer fear and hopelessness I felt that morning as we were called together and told of our leader's heart attack.

But the company then quickly deployed a very seasoned business leader from another part of the organization. The next day he held a team meeting and conveyed that calm presence in the face of chaos and adversity. He backed that up with decisive action and got everyone back to moving forward on the proposal. He knew exactly what to do and conveyed that calm assurance. We all began to pull ourselves together, and we won the rebid. That leader loaned to our group may have been worried and churning inside, but the calm he conveyed allowed our team to get going again.

INDEPENDENTLY RESPONSIBLE. Wise leaders are responsible for themselves and their actions. They own what occurs.

Many people may use words like "accountable" and "responsible" interchangeably. I see these as distinct concepts. I'll give my description of these concepts here. Credit for helping me see this distinction goes primarily to my coach, Jane Smith (Dorrier Underwood Consulting).

Accountability can be assigned to someone by someone else, and the person it is assigned to is then held accountable for accomplishing the assignment or result. Responsibility, on the other hand, cannot be assigned. Responsibility can only be chosen. A person has to choose for themselves to be responsible for something. A simple example: I can hold my son accountable for completing his schoolwork and achieving certain grades. I can create incentives, or disincentives, for encouraging performance. But only my son can choose for himself to be responsible for completing his schoolwork and producing results. When he is responsible, he now owns it. He is no longer an actor in my play; he has the lead role in his own play that he wrote, directed, produced, and stars in.

Being responsible for something can start with being held accountable for something, but it shifts when the person being held accountable <u>chooses</u> of his or her own accord to be independently responsible. When that shift occurs, the person is becoming wise.

A person being held accountable can be a victim— of circumstance, situation, other people, and so on. A responsible person is not a victim. The victim is playing a role in someone else's play. When freed from playing the role of victim in someone else's play, a person is now empowered to choose the role in his or her own play.

In every situation and result, a responsible person seeks out and chooses what part they play and what part they are responsible for. When something goes awry or produces a negative result, people involved often seek to blame others, point fingers, or claim they were a victim of circumstance in the role they played in the situation. You might hear them say, "Well, my part was fine, but . . ." or "The other department screwed up," or "This was out of my hands." A responsible person chooses what he or she is responsible for in the situation. That might sound more like "For my part in this, I could have done . . ." or "I take responsibility for not doing . . ." or "I am responsible for not raising this issue earlier."

A model I have seen for being independently responsible is the head football coach for my beloved alma mater, Clemson University. Early in his head coaching career at Clemson, Dabo Swinney had some success, but after a couple of years things seemed to be heading in the wrong direction. The offense had been producing fewer and fewer points and seemed to have no consistency and identity. After a mediocre season followed by a losing bowl game performance (which I witnessed in person, by the way), the coach held a press conference. As a rabid fan, I listened to the whole thing.

Many people wondered what he would say and do. He had a reputation of being loyal, friendly, and popular with his players and assistant coaches. Maybe he was not cut out for the tough things a head coach has to do. Was he up to making hard choices? Watching that press conference, I knew I would one day write about Dabo as a model for leadership. He stood and calmly said, "I am responsible for this. This is on me. The buck stops with me, and I will fix this." It may be that the university athletic director was planning to hold Dabo Swinney accountable for the situation, but instead Dabo chose to be responsible. He then went on to say that he was removing the offensive coordinator and was going to personally select a new one that fit his planned direction for the program.

In that act, he was firing a loyal assistant and friend. Dabo then went on to paint a new picture for a future of the football program at Clemson that rallied people to him.

As an executive, I understand the difficult decision he made and was inspired watching him convey it.

I'll give one counterexample to try to hit home this distinction of being independently responsible. I will use a political example, though this is not about partisan politics. I position it as a leadership (or lack thereof) example. In the aftermath of 9/11, the US foreign policy doctrine shifted to a doctrine of preemptive strike of credible, near-term threats to the US.

In invading Iraq in 2003, our leaders and their advisors believed that Iraq had developed weapons of mass destruction (WMDs). Numerous security analysts and policy makers were convinced that WMDs were being developed and stockpiled and readied for possible use against the West (or sale to other nefarious groups). It is factually known today that there were no WMDs in Iraq. None. We can debate all of the run-up to that decision, how decisions were made, and so forth, but I don't doubt that the president and his leaders truly believed WMDs existed. In the years since the Iraq invasion and the resulting chaos we created, some in President Bush's administration have taken partial responsibility for what was flawed data and a flawed decision and have expressed regret or reevaluation of the soundness of the decision to invade Iraq.

The sitting vice president at the time, however, has even recently still defiantly taken the stance that the invasion and subsequent decisions were good and justified, though WMDs have been proven not to exist. He has yet to say, "Here was my part in a bad decision," or "I was responsible for this not going well." However, he has been more than happy to claim credit for what he perceives as many positive outcomes. This is a classic example of a leader not being independently responsible. I think Gandalf would have said, "I made a bad decision, I take responsibility for that decision, and I will learn from it and not make that mistake again."

ORGANIZED. Another competency of *Individual Wisdom* is being organized. I don't mean that a wise leader has to have a clean desk, or no piles, or well-structured and labeled electronic files. These are helpful management and personal professional skills. I happen to have these skills well honed and it helps me be more efficient as a manager and professional, but that's not what I am talking about. From a leadership standpoint, "organized," as a way of being, is distinct.

Individual Wisdom includes being wise about prioritizing *time* (an irreplaceable resource), *people* (a hard-to-replace resource), and *money* (an easy-to-replace resource). It means having an organized mind that can see relationships, interconnections, and possible outcomes. It means having a sense of what combination of things works in a certain circumstance; it means working on the important things in work and life.

One of the key roles of a leader is to define and articulate what is important and what is not important or can wait and to organize around that. A wise leader also can see possibilities and consequences and organize around those to optimize both short term and long term. For example, as noted earlier, every leader must lead through adversity at some point. Some leaders get us through those adversities but only set us up for the next crisis and so we just survive from crisis to crisis. Wise leaders can see moves several steps ahead, knowing that once we get through this crisis, we'll need to be doing something else, and we can actually be positioning for that now.

In Tolkien's series, Gandalf's troupe experiences a series of existential crises, but you always have the sense that he is a few steps ahead, already ensuring that when they get through one crisis, they had better be positioned to handle the next. Gandalf also knows what is important and organizes around that. For example, he knows that the evil Gollum creature has been following them for a while and is a danger to them. When Frodo laments that they should have just killed him before, Gandalf articulates the possibility that Gollum likely has some important role to play in their futures. And this turns out to be true much later in the story.

And now to a real-world example. I mentioned in my introduction to this book that I worked for a time in corporate finance, and during that time I had the opportunity to work for the controller and later chief financial officer, David Walker. David was one of the brightest minds I ever worked with. He had flaws as a leader (as all of us do), but his mind could see several steps ahead at all times. He could see complex, multidimensional relationships and from that could focus his team on the most important things. David could connect seemingly unconnected things and predict with scary accuracy what would happen if we did or didn't take a particular action.

For example, he saw ahead to the relationships among our project cost inputs, debits and credits, corporate overheads, pricing competitiveness, regulatory frameworks, cash management, market dynamics, and share price. I think sometimes he actually manufactured crises because he felt like it focused his and his team's minds. We always came out of those crises better positioned to handle the next set of circumstances.

GENEROUS. The individually wise leader thinks of other individuals and organizations first. The classic example of this is the war fighter who gives of herself to save another or gives of himself to ensure freedom for the next generation. War always has a cost—in my opinion, often a cost greater than the resulting benefit. In the war example, the overall benefit (e.g., preserving freedom) may help a large number of people or countries. But that benefit will not be cashed in by everyone, even if it helps a large number of people. The war fighter who gives his life will never see the benefit. That cost is associated with generosity from someone for the good of another individual or something larger. So generosity is giving without expecting—or many times, receiving—a return.

In the business context, an individually wise leader gives his or her time freely to other individuals and institutions. As I note in other places in the book, I am coming to realize that time is the one irreplaceable resource. Not that I have discovered some amazing new insight for the world—many others have realized this before me and even written whole books about it. For me, as I settle into my fifties, I now get that concept of irreplaceable time at a more visceral level. So to give of your time is possibly the most generous thing you can do.

My mentor and friend Don Holzworth realized this concept after some years. Toward the end of his active career running companies, Don began spending significant time helping the University of North Carolina's School of Global Public Health. He has given plenty of money to the school, but those donations are fleeting and replaceable (though it's frequently not easy for an entrepreneur to part with his or her money!). As I note elsewhere, money is an easy-to-replace resource. What is irreplaceable is Don's time. Yet he spends many hours helping the school and, more important, mentoring students—the next generation of public health leaders.

A corollary of investing time to benefit others is freely sharing insights and experiences to help others achieve. You don't have to be north of fifty years old to have insights and experiences to share, though of course having those years on the earth helps. It doesn't even necessarily take a lot of time to share learning. What it takes is a willingness to help someone else's light to shine. To do this freely means anytime, anywhere, without anything expected in return.

My first boss, Frank O'Brien, the retired US Army lieutenant colonel, demonstrated this characteristic to me. In my early twenties, with a lot to prove and a ton of energy, I looked to Frank on how to channel that energy. Frank always had time and advice for me. Whenever I asked, or sometimes didn't ask, Frank offered his insights as shaped by his own experiences.

The Army tank Frank was commanding in Vietnam had been blown off a bridge, so most every other experience in life was not a big deal to him. His calm, low-key demeanor didn't fit the stereotype you might have of an Army colonel. He didn't push his ideas on me or demand I do certain things. He generally led me to figure out things on my own. Importantly, his way of being made it clear to me that he was not giving his insights so he could achieve more through me. It actually was about me and helping me achieve.

And that leads me to a third characteristic of generosity: the individually wise leader nurtures and contributes to others' ideas and initiatives without the need for credit. This could be because the leader has nothing else to prove, having achieved great things already. It could also be that the leader revels in seeing the success of others and knowing that he had some part to play in that success. Helping someone else succeed can be a tremendous energy rush. By the very nature of this characteristic, it is hard to pinpoint where the wise leader's contribution led to the success of another. Coming back to my first boss, Frank, and my early successes—winning new business, making a client happy, leading a small team—Frank contributed to all of those for me. He put me forward rather than himself.

One of the key elements of being a thought leader is mentoring others, including helping others get published without need of taking credit. We'll explore this more in Chapter 4, *Thought Leadership*. The ultimate generosity for a thought leader is helping someone else get published but not putting the thought leader's name on it.

SUMMARY COMMENTS

In summary, *Individual Wisdom* is about being on the journey of self-actualization. The competencies I have defined in *Individual Wisdom* are: curiosity, continuous learning, self-confidence, courageous, cool under pressure, independently responsible, organized, and generous.

To know others, you must first know yourself; to lead others, you must first be able to lead yourself. *Individual Wisdom* is the linchpin of the entire Complete Business Leader framework. *Individual Wisdom*—the self-actualized leader—unleashes the possibility for a leader to develop all of the other dimensions of the framework. Throughout the rest of the book, you'll notice that I refer back to competencies and specific behaviors of *Individual Wisdom*, with many specific examples of different leaders either demonstrating or not demonstrating these aspects of *Individual Wisdom*. With these cross-references I am hoping to demonstrate the interconnected nature of the Complete Business Leader and, critically, how the aspects of *Individual Wisdom* enable a leader to be effective in other dimensions of the Complete Business Leader.

In other chapters, I'll also make reference to leaders in business, art, politics, and the military who exhibit various aspects of this interconnectedness of *Individual Wisdom* to other dimensions of becoming a Complete Business Leader. Specifically, I will refer to Dwight Eisenhower, who over a lifelong leadership journey became increasingly wise and increasingly complete.

Of course, the leader who *knows* she is on the journey of *Individual Wisdom knows* she has not arrived—and never will—but *knows* that being increasingly self-aware, increasingly wise, serves as the pathway lighting to access other dimensions of the Complete Business Leader, and it is through these other dimensions that the leader achieves results.

> Leaders cause things to happen that weren't just going to happen anyway.
> **—Unknown**

Competency	Example Behavior
Curiosity	o Exhibits interest and openness to reexamining previously held beliefs and views o Asks lots of questions
Continuous learning	o Is driven to continually develop, grow, and improve o Reads and studies constantly o Actively seeks out new knowledge
Self-confidence	o Is willing to be vulnerable o Doesn't make excuses and takes responsibility for mistakes o Creates solutions rather than being a victim of circumstances
Courageous	o Displays courage in making hard decisions, having hard conversations, and taking on hard tasks o Goes to the source to solve problems o Acts in spite of fears
Cool under pressure	o Handles ambiguity and uncertainty well o Exhibits calm, clear thinking in the face of chaos or adversity
Independently responsible	o Takes on being the source of what happens o Self-empowers by choosing paths rather than waiting for them to be chosen
Organized	o Prioritizes time, people, and financial resources o Defines what is important and what is not important
Generous	o Invests time freely in individuals and institutions, giving back to others who need it o Freely shares wisdom, insights, and experiences to help others achieve o Nurtures and contributes to others' ideas and initiatives without need for credit

RELATIONSHIP MANAGEMENT

Winston Churchill and Franklin D. Roosevelt changed the trajectory of the world through their relationship. Many books have been written about Churchill and about Roosevelt separately or about Roosevelt, Churchill, and Stalin together as a triumvirate. But few authors have focused specifically on the complex, nuanced relationship of Roosevelt and Churchill. Jon Meacham's book *Franklin and Winston: An Intimate Portrait of an Epic Friendship* does that.

> Like most friends Churchill and Roosevelt were sometimes affectionate,
> sometimes cross, alternately ready to die for or murder each other.
> But each helped make what the other did possible.
> **— Jon Meacham**

Complete Business Leaders create long-term, mutually beneficial relationships based on trust and mutual respect. Now let's unpack those attributes a bit:

Long-term—This implies two things. First, a real relationship takes a while to nurture and fully bloom, so it is long term in its development. Second, a real relationship lasts for the long term; it is durable over the arc of time.

Mutually beneficial—This implies that both parties and their individual and common interests benefit from the relationship.

Trust—This is self-evident, but just to be clear, this means that each party believes the other individual and the relationship itself can be relied on. The relationship itself is founded on and operates from this belief.

Mutual respect—This implies each individual respects and exhibits respect for the other individual and the relationship itself. This plays out in honoring the other's point of view, even if the person disagrees with it. It means authentically wanting the best for the other person and for the relationship.

Roosevelt and Churchill's relationship exhibited all four of these attributes.

It was long term. They met first just after the end of WWI, but their relationship developed in earnest in the late 1930s as the world increasingly was turned upside down by Hitler's military aggression and the resulting deterioration of order in Europe.[2] The relationship deepened and evolved until the time of Roosevelt's death in the spring of 1945.

The relationship was mutually beneficial. Churchill and Roosevelt were very different people with different personas, leadership styles, and political skills. In many ways, they completed each other and made each other better. In the late 1930s, Churchill desperately needed Roosevelt and the US. He courted and nurtured their relationship persistently.[3] As Great Britain became the last European holdout against Hitler, the urgency of relationship became all consuming for Churchill. Roosevelt, too, needed Churchill. Roosevelt knew that the US and the American people must reengage on the world stage before it was too late, both in Europe and in the Pacific.

Churchill and Great Britain, with their long interconnected histories to the American people, gave impetus to Roosevelt's push for America to reengage in the world.[4] Through the course of the relationship and the war, that relationship continued to be mutually beneficial, each needing the other and each benefiting from the partnership.

The relationship was built on trust. Each generally trusted the other's motives and long-term desires. And while they many times squabbled and disagreed on things, they could anchor themselves back in their trust of each other and their institutional trust in their respective nations.[5] As with any relationship, trust is sometimes broken, but once set as the benchmark, Roosevelt and Churchill fell back on that trust consistently. They were able to rebuild the trust when it was broken.

Their relationship was based on mutual respect. This mutual respect was for each other as individuals and for the nations they represented. Churchill and Roosevelt demonstrated an understanding of each other's strengths and positions. Churchill knew and acknowledged that Roosevelt was a shrewd, sophisticated politician and a visionary thinker. Roosevelt knew and acknowledged that Churchill was a tremendous orator and had an infectious, gregarious personality.[6] Sometimes they acted in ways that were inconsistent with that mutual respect, but they quickly repaired it. Roosevelt and Churchill also understood that they were a far more powerful and compelling force together than alone in leading the Allies to confront and eventually defeat Nazi Germany.

In the rest of this chapter, I'll describe the key competencies of *Relationship Management* for the Complete Business Leader, again using some real-world examples I have seen and experienced to anchor this conceptual discussion in reality. And since their relationship captures the essence of what I mean by relationship management, from time to time I'll refer back to the Churchill-Roosevelt relationship.

One other note: I realize that "managing" a relationship might sound a bit manipulative or selfish, so you could suggest that this dimension of the Complete Business Leader framework be more appropriately titled "relationship nurturing" or "relationship development," and that would be fine. However, I thought about this quite a bit, and I actually like the characteristics that the word "management" implies, like being systematic, disciplined, intentional, and planful. Those aspects can actually help ensure that a relationship is lasting, is built on trust and mutual respect, and produces mutually rewarding results. I think you will see that as we progress through the rest of this chapter.

COMPETENCIES OF RELATIONSHIP MANAGEMENT

Below I describe seven competencies and example behaviors that form the basis for Complete Business Leaders to create and manage relationships.

INSTITUTIONAL REPRESENTATION. In most business settings, you are representing both yourself and your organization in a relationship. Relationships are, by their nature, personal, but also can involve the personification of institutions and organizations. So one of the key competencies of effective *Relationship Management* in a business context is representing your institution well.

A CEO colleague of mine once told me a story once about a company he ran for a founder-owner. The owner said to him (paraphrasing): "I only want three things from you as my CEO: do some good in the world, make me some money, and don't f***ing embarrass me." With that directive, my CEO friend had a pretty clear view of how to represent his institution in relationships out in the world.

In institutional representation, you are personifying the needs, expectations, and values of your organization. At the same time, just underneath the surface are your own individual needs, expectations, and values. This all works better if the institutional ethos is in sync with the individual ethos. It is also important for a leader to know which of these two he is projecting at any given time and understand any distinctions between the two.

To illuminate this point, let's go back to the Churchill-Roosevelt example. Clearly each was representing his own country, but their individual personalities, values, and notions also got projected through that relationship. Each personified both the admirable and not so admirable aspects of their country's culture. For example, Churchill personified and projected his country's old-world colonial views about India, Africa, and other controlled peoples of the British Empire. Roosevelt personified and projected his country's upstart and sometimes unrealistic enthusiasm for how quickly geopolitical change could happen.[7] Each clearly knew how to both represent his country, anchored with their individual personas, and find ways forward that were mutually beneficial.

In a position of organizational leadership, you rarely get to "take off the clothes" of your organization. In every interaction, every business and social setting, you are the personification of your organization. Sometimes I have seen leaders struggle with maintaining this alignment. Because we are human, we fail. We don't always live up to our individually declared values or those of our organization. But it's especially poignant for executive leaders. Whether we as leaders like it or not, others both inside and outside of the company are looking at us *as the company.*

Here is a real-world example. Some years ago at Constella Group, we zoned in on our core purpose as a company, which was about "enhancing human health around the world, every day." We decided that it would be incongruent with that purpose if we allowed the vending machines with terrible processed junk foods to stay in our building. So we removed the vending machines. From the staff's angry reaction, you would have thought we had slashed salaries by 25 percent. Furthermore, in our executive team meetings, we started serving only healthy breakfasts, snacks, and lunches. Several of us, myself included, just wanted to "take off our organizational clothes" and eat a bag of Doritos in public once in a while.

TAKING THE LONG VIEW. Great relationship managers see relationships over a long arc of time. They seek to build connection first, with no ask or expectation of immediate return. And that connection has to be real, not contrived. That connection has to be grounded in creating a relationship that is a new thing—one that is more than the two individuals separately and one that exists outside of institutions to which each belongs. If the relationship exists and grows only because of their two institutional identities, then the relationship may wither once their institutions affiliations change. Real relationships, those that are rooted in trust and mutual respect, take time and energy. Great relationship managers in a business context expend real energy and time and don't expect or require a payoff.

The Churchill-Roosevelt relationship took the long view. As early as 1933, Churchill began courting and nurturing the relationship with Roosevelt, sending books and other gifts to FDR and writing him letters. For years, Churchill got little to nothing back out of his efforts. Roosevelt generally ignored him.[8] But Churchill had a persistence, tenacity, and an intentionality to develop a relationship with Roosevelt. And so he did.

As I mentioned in the introduction chapter, Don Holzworth, my long-time colleague and CEO at Constella Group, was a master at relationship management. For literally years, he nurtured relationships with banks, private equity firms, and other much larger companies. Early on, he asked for nothing, but he learned from them while they learned about the market from him. When the time eventually came that Don wanted to sell the company, many of those relationships paid off. We had bankers, private equity firms, and other larger companies beating down our door to buy the company.

In fact, Don used to push me to spend more energy networking and relationship building externally than operationally managing internally. He used to counsel me that anytime I traveled to our other offices, I should set a goal of spending the majority of each day *outside* the office rather than inside it. I didn't fully appreciate that advice until I was CEO of Futures Group.

Over the course of six years as CEO of Futures Group, I built a substantial network of external business colleagues and friends who would eventually become target banks, private equity sponsors, business partners, board members, key hires, and acquisition candidates. And when I left Futures at the beginning of 2015 to start my new venture, almost immediately fellow CEO colleagues came calling, wanting my consulting help or to hire me; bankers and private equity firms were happy to hear my business plans and back me; and other partners were interested in helping me.

Another old boss and friend, John Cook, modeled this long view of relationships for me. I worked for John at BDM back in the mid-1990s. John liked to go out and smoke cigars and drink good wine with people. Back then, I enjoyed the wine but didn't realize how what John was doing was intentional. John knew almost as second nature that results are accomplished only with people, and that requires long-term trusted relationships. He was not a "technical" person per se, but John had mastery of developing and maintaining long-term trusted relationships. It was a systematic, rigorously applied competency, just as any other technical skill.

I left BDM at the end of 1998. After I left, and mostly from John's impetus initially, we maintained a relationship. That relationship actually deepened after we were not working together anymore. Over the years, we got together regularly and talked about business, markets, families, and what kind of difference we wanted to make in the world. Whenever we were traveling and in the same city, we tried to meet up for one of our long dinners—with, of course, good wine. We advised each other, made contacts for each other, shared our hopes and dreams, and genuinely connected as human beings. In the end, John had probably left exactly the legacy he intended: he passed on to a new generation of leaders like me the value of long-term relationships.

CREATING COMMON GROUND. Every leader—every human being, really—has to negotiate frequently with other individuals or institutions. Complete Business Leaders are great negotiators. They don't create win-lose situations. They don't just "find" common ground on which to compromise; rather, they "create" new ground by enlarging the conversation with new possibility. Negotiation for Complete Business Leaders is a generative process, making both sides more whole.

Never was this more true than in the creation of the United Nations as WWII was coming to a close. Roosevelt, Churchill, and Stalin together invented something new, a construct that was intended to avoid ever having another world war. For over sixty years now, this construct has worked, though some people with isolationist views still seek to diminish or dismantle the UN.[9] Roosevelt, Churchill, Stalin, their secondary allies, and their staffs worked ceaselessly until they created something that was distinct from anything the world had seen before.

Of course, this endeavor involved hundreds of compromises on all sides, but all of those small compromises were subordinate in comparison to creating the common ground as they did. In the end, these leaders created a new institution they could all support and get behind. And more, they invented a new world order, a whole new way for the world to work that included constructs for resolving differences peacefully, having all voices heard, preserving territorial integrity, and governing bilateral and multilateral relationships.

> The Charter of the United Nations which you have just signed is a solid structure upon which we can build a better world. History will honor you for it.
>
> **—President Harry Truman**

Roosevelt did not live to see the consummation of their bold ideas. He died in April before the UN Charter was signed in San Francisco in June 1945. He did not get to witness the 850 delegates from fifty nations come together to create common ground.[10] But it surely would not have happened without the relationship between Roosevelt and Churchill.

Most leaders will never encounter opportunity where the stakes are quite as high as creating a new world order, but the kind of commitment, energy, and persistence required to do so can yield tremendous progress in any organizational setting.

MUTUAL RESPECT. Another competency of relationship management is mutual respect. This can be exhibited by a range of outward behaviors, including setting and continually reconfirming mutual expectations and pushing back respectfully on unreasonable requests when needed.

I was once in a client meeting in Atlanta where my team was being "taken to the woodshed." The client asked me to show up as the senior accountable executive. The project was not going well from the client's perspective. My team felt like the expectations for success were continually shifting on them and that there was nothing they could do that would make this particular client happy—almost as if the client were setting them up for failure.

Sound familiar? Almost every business leader has encountered this. Just as I was weighing in my mind how best to respond in order to both respect the client's view and defend my team, another executive who worked for me and had accompanied me to the meeting jumped in. This other colleague and I had a sometimes stormy relationship, and we butted heads frequently. In fact, I originally was not going to bring him to the meeting because I was uncertain of how he would conduct himself in the meeting. But in this instance, I was mesmerized at how he deftly handled the situation.

It turned out he knew that client better than I did and had an already established level of mutual respect. He also knew the subject matter specifics of the project better than I. He took responsibility (see Chapter 2, *Individual Wisdom*) where our team had not delivered, and then he pushed back on some aspects where the client had not upheld their end, including timely reviews and getting us certain information we needed. In a respectful way, he called the client out. My colleague was able to do this because he and the client already had that established level of respect. He then led us all through a resetting of expectations and a way forward. In this exchange, my colleague not only leveraged the existing mutual respect but actually reinforced and further built that respect going forward.

Another characteristic of building and maintaining mutual respect is giving bad news early. It may seem like an obvious thing to do but is surprisingly hard, and even seasoned leaders have a hard time doing this. Giving another business colleague, whether a client, a boss, a partner, or staff, bad news earlier rather than later actually demonstrates respect for the other individual. It demonstrates you care about and respect the other person enough to make yourself vulnerable, to risk disappointing or angering them or even damaging their respect for you.

I haven't met many people who enjoyed giving bad news. And I certainly don't either, though I have had to give my share of bad news. I've had to fire people I really liked, tell an external partner no, tell a boss we missed our numbers, and tell a client we screwed up. I have found it works to ask myself, would I rather have this person hear this news from me now or from someone else later? And do I honor and respect the person enough to overcome my reticence and give them this news?

Demonstrating mutual respect also involves having hard conversations of all kinds. I have felt this most often in having frank conversations with staff about their performance when they have not met my expectations. Again, for some leaders, this type of conversation may come easy, but I know from countless discussions with other leaders, for even accomplished leaders, this is one of the most difficult things they have to do.

I still remember one conversation I had to have with a senior executive who worked for me. I was about forty years old, and he was close to sixty and a former military flag officer. We had bought his company and he remained on in a business development capacity, working now for me. He was a positive, likeable person. Clients liked him and my other leaders enjoyed being around him. Yet over time he was not producing the business growth results we needed. It was difficult for me on many levels to have the performance conversations I had with him over many months, eventually leading to the dreaded conversation of having to let him go.

I rehearsed that conversation multiple times with my executive coach. She kept reminding me that I was actually demonstrating respect for him as a person and a professional by telling him the truth. I was treating him as an adult worthy of respect by telling him he was not delivering results, even after multiple coaching discussions. That last conversation was, in fact, very difficult. But we had an amicable, respectful parting. If anything, I think the experience made him more determined in the future— he decided he was not yet ready to retire and landed with another company—and gave me clarity on how to anchor having hard conversations in mutual respect.

ENGAGEMENT. No matter whether you are in a tech company, a government agency, or a church, leadership requires engaging with others, at least until the age of droids comes and robots can accomplish all work endeavors with no need of human beings! Complete Business Leaders engage others. Engagement involves human-to-human contact: genuine dialogue, intentional listening, authentic empathy, and committed problem-solving.

In the Churchill War Rooms underneath 10 Downing Street, Churchill had a special encrypted phone installed in a private small closet with insulated walls.[11] This was his Roosevelt phone. This is where he went to have completely private one-to-one conversations with Roosevelt. As good friends and colleagues as Roosevelt and Churchill were, they had to regularly engage.

When they experienced long periods of not seeing each other or speaking by phone, their relationship was not as strong. They would sometimes start wondering about each other's actions and motives. Why did Franklin make that decision? Why did Winston make that statement to the press? But every time they spoke or saw each other—truly engaged with each other—that relationship was renewed. Human to human. Both of them were intentional about ensuring they engaged regularly.

As noted in Richard Holmes's biography of Churchill, Roosevelt and Churchill sent to each other over seventeen hundred letters and telegrams during the war years, and this number doesn't capture the numerous other informal phone calls they had, and of course in person visits.[12] Frequently, of course, Roosevelt and Churchill's engagement was about the execution of the war, but it was grounded in their relationship. Many times their conversations were about mundane things and sometimes about deeply personal things. And sometimes about "work"—running countries and prosecuting wars.

Rich Cohn, a superb leader with whom I had the privilege to work for a number of years, exhibited exactly what I mean by "engagement." Rich was a peer leader and eventually ended up working for me. He was a PhD statistician, yet he schooled me in engagement. He engaged in genuine back and forth dialogue, whether talking with an employee about their daughter's school choices or working with other statisticians on his team to design a new research protocol. He was an intentional listener; he asked great questions (and really *heard* the answers), let others talk a lot, and sought to learn through listening. He was authentically empathetic; you sensed he was seeing the world, and the issue at hand, through your vantage point—that he was standing in your world with your concerns, notions, and views.

The reason I say "authentic" is because there are many who have learned communication techniques to *sound* empathetic with their questions but in the end are not really standing in your world with you. Rich was committed to finding solutions together to problems. His analytical nature aided him here in being a natural problem solver, breaking down the issues, studying the data at hand, identifying roadblocks, and working with you to create a solution. In short, he was fully engaged with you. You felt like you were in the same game with him—on the same team, in fact. By the way, his way of engaging with me did not shift at all when I became his boss. He was just the same.

RESPONSIVENESS. Another aspect of effective relationship management is responsiveness. This is a bit ironic, considering today's communication context of near instantaneous texts, tweets, and emails. And of course, it may seem blatantly obvious that you should respond in a timely way to others, particularly clients. What I am talking about here, though, is responsiveness as a *way of being*. Being responsive to others sets a tone in a relationship that you respect and honor the other person and the relationship itself.

Complete Business Leaders manage relationships by being responsive. They make it a priority to respond quickly to emails, phone calls, and any other communication medium available. Everybody gets tons of emails. Everybody is busy and stretched. Everybody has important things they are doing. I completely reject the notion that someone is "too busy to respond." What that really says is that someone didn't make it a *priority* to respond. Responding could even be just a quick one-line email or text back acknowledging (read *respecting*) the other person and saying, "I got your note and will get you a more full response in the next twenty-four hours."

Referring back to Don Holzworth, his total way of being was responsive. He was so quick triggered on email, calls, etc., that he sometimes screwed up with his messaging, but you never had to worry about a note languishing with Don. He always moved the action forward. Don was running a $200 million business, concurrently serving on half a dozen boards, investing in other startups, and flying around the country to support his son's budding golf career.

Contrast that with another business colleague who worked for me for many years. He was a brilliant business mind and a friend, but he was utterly terrible at being responsive. He was an equal opportunity nonresponder. Peers, his staff, his boss, even clients and external partners were all disrespected. Daily. Though this colleague's intention was not disrespect, that is what people were left with. My colleague had virtually no outside interests or activities, and though he did have an executive-level role, he wasn't running the company. Given my colleague's unresponsiveness, you would have thought he had Don's sort of responsibilities and schedule.

So it's not about how busy or important you are. It's about a *way of being* responsive that demonstrates respect for relationships. To this day, though Don is long done running companies, he remains extremely active; he has his fingers into many things, *and* he remains reliably responsive.

Responsiveness means being attentive to helping others when they need it, whether they ask for it or not. It also means helping when there is nothing coming in return, no quid pro quo. Being intentional about building relationships means when someone needs something, you find a way to help.

As I have gotten older, I have had increasing opportunities to help others—not because I want anything in return but because I genuinely want to build relationships and be responsive to others' needs. This includes, for example, taking the time to meet with grad students to hear about their career hopes and dreams and finding ways to help connect them into the professional community (refer back to generosity from Chapter 2, *Individual Wisdom*).

Here is how this manifests as responsiveness: If I get an email or other request to meet with a grad student, I respond that day if at all possible. I think there may be a tendency to prioritize, among a set of emails that a business leader needs to respond to, and put a "lowly" grad student at the bottom of the list. I say the Complete Business Leader who is responsive puts the grad student high on the priority list. If your way of being is responsive, then it doesn't matter whether the person you need to respond to is a grad student, a vendor, a colleague, or a board member.

STANDING FOR THE OTHER. When you are standing for someone, you genuinely want and seek the best for that person, no strings attached. Complete Business Leaders are able to truly forget about themselves and stand for someone else. Standing for someone else builds relationship and connection with that person. As a definitional sidenote: Standing for the other is different from standing *up* for them. Standing *up* for someone makes you responsible, not them. Standing *for* someone empowers that someone and lets them be responsible.

> Connection is why we are here. It gives meaning and purpose to our lives.
> **—Brené Brown, Author**

My executive coach, Jane Smith, stood for me. It's clear to me that when she sat down with me, she stepped into my world and it was no longer about her. It was about me and her helping me fulfill all my hopes and dreams. Sometimes that involved asking me hard questions—ones that I didn't really want to address. Or holding up the mirror to me on how I was occurring.

Sometimes wanting the best for someone involves giving them feedback, not only uncomfortable but feedback they really don't want. It is up to the receiver to do something with that feedback, but wanting the best for the other calls us to offer the feedback. Sometimes my kids have not wanted or liked my feedback. I am very clear now, though, that my giving them feedback is a way of standing for them. It is not about me or what I want or expect. It's about helping them with the opportunity to become their best selves.

My good friend and colleague, Alonzo Fulgham, stands for me. He persistently calls me to be more than I even think I could be, even if I am tired and don't want to be. He also stands for others. For more than thirty years, Alonzo has stood for his professional colleagues. He is known as someone who would do anything for you with no expectation of return for himself. As a result, he has a vast network of people literally around the world who dearly love him and feel connected to him.

A couple of years ago, I had the opportunity to actually make a connection for him. I introduced him to another colleague of mine when I thought they could be beneficial to each other. Of course, I expected nothing in return. Alonzo was greatly appreciative but, more important, it gave me the opportunity to tell him I learned that way of standing for someone else from him.

SUMMARY COMMENTS

For some leaders, building relationships with others is like breathing; for others, it is work. For all leaders who are on the journey to being complete, it is essential. As I have described above, Complete Business Leaders create long-term, mutually beneficial relationships based on trust and mutual respect.

I've broken down how I think about relationship management, based on my own experiences, into component competencies, all of which can be learned and developed even if they do not come naturally: Institutional representation, Taking the long view, Creating common ground, Mutual respect, Engagement, Responsiveness, and Standing for the other.

You'll see me refer multiple times later in the book to Dwight Eisenhower. Eisenhower, of course, was a contemporary of Churchill and Roosevelt. As supreme commander of the Allied forces in Europe, his role was quite different than Churchill and Roosevelt, but he interacted with them frequently and was masterful at managing a myriad of complex and nuanced personal, political, and military relationships. He interacted with his Russian/Soviet counterparts as well.[13]

Eisenhower demonstrated all of the *Relationship Management* competencies I have documented above in his role in Europe. He represented his country but, more important, was able to represent *all* of the Allies. He was successful in his role, in part, because he was viewed by the Allies as more than just the US commander. They believed he was *standing for them*, not just his own country. He took the time to *engage* all key stakeholders, hear them out, and find *common ground*, even with the Russians.

At the core of each of the *Relationship Management* competencies (and linked to the CBL dimension in Chapter 2, *Individual Wisdom*) is a commitment to and authentic caring for other human beings. Only with this commitment and caring can you *know* other human beings, meaning knowing who they are or want to be; what their needs and desires are, spoken and unspoken; and what is important to them and why. Engaging with other human beings to accomplish things together requires intentionality in managing relationships.

> Meeting Franklin Roosevelt was like opening your first
> bottle of Champagne; knowing him was like drinking it.
> **—Winston Churchill**

Competency	Example Behavior
Institutional representation	o Represents the organization and its values, serving as an ambassador for the organization o Identifies and understands individual and institutional needs and concerns
Taking the long view	o Builds connections with no expectation of immediate return
Building common ground	o Expands and invents possibilities o Seeks mutually beneficial solutions and gains agreement, including scope, budgets, and responsibilities
Mutual respect	o Sets and continually reaffirms mutual expectations o Respectfully pushes back on unreasonable requests and finds ways forward for both parties o Delivers bad news early but with a corrective action plan
Engagement	o Presents ideas and advice clearly o Actively and regularly engages in dialogue o Serves as a problem solver and solution provider
Responsiveness	o Documents client/partner interactions o Is highly responsive via email, calls, and other communications
Standing for the other	o Genuinely seeks the best for another person o Sacrifices self for the interest of others

THOUGHT LEADERSHIP

Back where I come from, we have universities, seats of great learning,

where men go to become great thinkers. And when they come out,

they think deep thoughts and with no more brains than you have.

But they have one thing you haven't got: a diploma.

—The Wizard, L. Frank Baum's *The Wonderful Wizard of Oz*

What might the Scarecrow have said about thought leadership? The straw-stuffed scarecrow from the Wizard of Oz didn't even have a brain, or so he believed. And he didn't have a diploma to prove he was a great thinker. But I think we could say over the course of the story, Scarecrow developed into a thought leader.

The term "thought leader" is bandied all around in modern business parlance. Many consulting organizations have designated thought leaders or thought leadership initiatives. Science-based, academically oriented companies and nonprofits typically promote their thought leadership in certain areas.

My working definition of a thought leader—a recognized and sought-after expert in a professional field—is generally consistent with the common interpretation in today's professional communities globally. Underneath the general definition, I have a specific take on the competencies and characteristics of *Thought Leadership*. I'll describe those in some detail and, as with other CBL competencies, provide real-world examples as we go through the chapter. And occasionally I might even throw in a reference to our strawman.

Now you might ask, why do I think *Thought Leadership* is a pillar of being a Complete *Business* Leader? That's a fair question. Why would a businessperson need to be a thought leader? I have heard many managers and executives say something like, "I am not the expert. I just hire great people and give them the resources they need to do their job." I concur that a key skill of successful executives is the ability to hire great people and align resources (in fact, see later CBL chapters devoted to these areas), but my own experience is that in our new global knowledge economy, the Complete Business Leader can't just be a good manager of people and resources.

It's no longer sufficient for the leader to be ignorant of anything other than general management principles. The complete leader needs to be a technical expert in one or more areas as well. This thought leadership engenders respect and credibility both internally and externally, allowing the leader to attract and rally talent internally and build market presence and brand externally. And it provides gravitas for the leader to make the hard decisions when needed.

The technical expert without the broader leadership dimensions is just a clanging instrument in the empty forest. The broad-based general manager with no recognized technical expertise to trade on is like the king everyone mocks behind his back. Not all but many great kings first developed skill as warriors. Historically this was viewed as critically important for a king to be a good enough warrior to inspire and lead his people.

Expertise may be in medicine, biology, IT, or other areas typically recognized as "technical," and I propose that this expertise could also be in typically administrative areas such as finance, human resources, and project management. My rule of thumb on what could comprise thought leadership is this: *any* professional skill area that can be categorized as a learned discipline with a body of knowledge, professional associations, and training and certifications, where one is compensated differentially for that expertise, qualifies as an area of possible thought leadership.

For example, a CFO could be a thought leader in corporate finance and accounting. This represents a learned discipline you study in school; there are professional associations, such as the AICPA; there are special continuing education and certification expectations, such as the CPA certification; and there is differential compensation for a CFO.

You might be interested to know that I actually incorporated this *Thought Leadership* dimension into the CBL framework much later than other dimensions, after the framework was already in practice in an organization. So it was not in my original thinking. Augmenting the CBL by adding an entirely new dimension was part of my natural expansion and evolution as I continue to learn myself.

This new learning is due in part to my time with Futures Group. My good friend and colleague Farley Cleghorn helped me reevaluate the Complete Business Leader framework and sketch out what the dimension of *Thought Leadership* looked like. And Farley would know. He embodies thought leadership.

An infectious disease physician researcher by training and practice, Farley became one of the world's recognized experts in HIV/AIDS and has dedicated his life's work to prevention and treatment of HIV/AIDS. Farley was my chief technical officer at Futures Group and thus oversaw the technical delivery of all of our programs and contracts, ensuring the highest caliber technical delivery. He was—still is—recognized both internally and externally as a thought leader. Farley is a magnet for securing funding from clients, connecting with partners, and attracting other talented experts. And key technical talent is the essential ingredient to a successful professional services and consulting business.

One of the interesting dynamics of the *Thought Leadership* dimension is that it can be learned and developed. There are people with lots of letters after their names who are not thought leaders. And there are lots of people who have no letters after their names who are thought leaders.

A thought leader doesn't just declare one day that he or she is a thought leader. A thought leader is referred to that way by others, particularly the external world. It's a part of someone's personal brand. So, if you can't just declare one day that you are a thought leader, how do you get others to declare that about you?

COMPETENCIES OF THOUGHT LEADERSHIP

In my work, I have found there are three primary competencies involved in *Thought Leadership* in the context of becoming a Complete Business Leader. A thought leader is: active externally, an innovator, and active internally. Below I will describe each of these three and highlight a set of behaviors, or characteristics, that demonstrate that competency. As usual, I'll sprinkle in real-world examples from my own experience, as well as what I have observed elsewhere.

ACTIVE EXTERNALLY. A thought leader has to be active externally, out interacting in the professional world. A professional who sits in his office all day can't possibly be a thought leader. A thought leader shares what she knows with the outside world. Being active externally includes taking leadership roles in professional societies, working groups, and committees; being recognized by peers; speaking and publishing; and exciting the market with new ideas and concepts. All of this takes more than just a couple years and a couple of committees or speaking engagements.

As noted earlier, I have intentionally tried to stay somewhat broad in my career, but in each market segment I have worked, I have needed to develop enough technical credibility to be able to operate as a business leader in that field. For years, I have dabbled in the life sciences research industry. For a time, I even ran a contract research organization (CRO) services business unit that managed clinical trials globally for pharmaceutical companies.

With intentionality, I worked to gain at least some measure of technical credibility and knowledge so that people I was managing, selling to, or interacting with couldn't just dismiss me with "You don't understand our industry." I dove into the life sciences industry with gusto, went to conferences, started getting speaking engagements, got myself plugged into committees, and ended up chairing a national steering group on clinical data management. After several years of intense and intentional preparation, I was becoming known in the pharma market as an expert in clinical data management. Evidence of that fact is I was awarded the Drug Information Association's Outstanding Service award in 2007 (DIA is the main global industry association for the pharma clinical trials market).

Had I become a thought leader? I would say I was heading that direction but probably needed some additional pieces— like ten more years of involvement as described above, like publishing additional groundbreaking ideas and approaches, like having a broader recognition globally. Also, I probably would have had to abandon my numerous other obligations back in the public sector side of our business. But I was never willing to walk away from my other worlds and really spend the time and energy needed to become a true thought leader in pharma clinical data management. On the Complete Business Leader pilgrimage, the leader can't become single faceted.

Ron Fitzmartin, on the other hand, *is* a thought leader in the field of clinical trials and data management. Now a senior official at FDA, Ron has devoted his entire career to the study of clinical data management methods and approaches. In that field, Ron is universally known and is generally one of the first names off of someone's lips if they are looking for a credible source. Ron actually invested in me by helping me get plugged into the right committees and speaking engagements and was a good colleague and mentor in navigating the pharma clinical data management community. It's actually Chapter 3, the *Relationship Management* dimension of the Complete Business Leader model, that I displayed in connecting with Ron and developing a strong relationship.

John Stover is a also thought leader. John was one of the early employees of Futures Group back in the early 1970s. I first came to know John when Constella Group acquired

Futures Group in early 2005. Soon after the acquisition, John approached us with a proposal to divest a small group of employees back out as an independent company. Being part of a bigger company was just not interesting to him. We negotiated a deal to let him do that, and so John started a new company that has stayed small, focused, and true to John's professional passions. That organization, called Avenir Health, is considered the go-to organization in several specialty areas of the global development market. The company is connected to John's personal brand in the market.

Though he never actually completed his PhD, John is considered one of the world's leaders in family planning and HIV modeling and forecasting for developing countries. He is highly published. If you go to almost any publication or set of statistics on world and country population growth and its effects on other demographic dynamics, such as population health, education, economic growth, and climate, you'll most likely see John Stover's name associated with the study.

Another example of being active externally is another longtime friend and colleague, Jesse Milan Jr. Now a bit over sixty years old with distinguished graying hair, Jesse is a thought leader in HIV/AIDS. He is recognized by his peers as a thought leader, one with moral authority. Jesse has many leadership qualities but focuses primarily on his life's work and experience in HIV/AIDS advocacy, calling for more funding, better policies, and better prevention and treatment services, especially for marginalized communities in the United States.

Jesse has spent almost his entire career devoted to these causes. Jesse speaks in broad strokes and with a huge stage persona—big physical motions, soaring language, and an infectious smile. Besides being a gifted public speaker, Jesse's "street cred" comes from the fact that he has been living with HIV for more than thirty years now. He contracted the virus in the early 1980s and experienced the personal loss of his partner and many other friends in that era. Though he has done this advocacy work in various roles and organizations, he has stayed true to his purpose.

A thought leader needs to not just be active in the professional community speaking and publishing; the thought leader needs to excite the market and create buzz.

Another colleague of mine does that in the area of innovative technologies for health. Bobby Jefferson is frequently on the speaking circuit and serves on innovation and social entrepreneur panels. He brings buzz. He brings creativity and innovative ideas to virtually every setting. And he has a communication style that brings these tech ideas down to an understandable layperson level. Bobby has mastered the art of wowing non-techies—not by showing how smart or knowledgeable he is but rather by demonstrating how technology can change the trajectory of peoples' lives in the everyday.

People flock to hear him speak. I once had Bobby speak at a breakfast series that typically drew twenty to thirty people to hear a speaker on a global health topic. We were always looking for ways to get more people to show up, even convincing ourselves that it was perhaps just too early in the day for people to come. When I put Bobby on the schedule with his topic of mobile health technology innovations in the developing world, we packed the room.

Jesse Milan Jr., John Stover, and Bobby Jefferson couldn't be more different stylistically, but they are all thought leaders who are active externally. You don't have to be singularly focused and world famous, but you need a niche, a hook where you are very comfortable and credible.

INNOVATOR. A second competency thought leaders must have is they must be innovators. Over the years as I have studied and spoken on innovation, I have come to some of my own definitions around innovation. There is no one authoritative definition, but here is mine: innovation is the creation of the new *and* the needed. Let me unpack that a bit. "Creation" is a powerful word. It implies action. It implies something exists now that didn't exist before, at least not in that form. As I already noted under the *Individual Wisdom* dimension, Complete Business Leaders are creative. They create or cause things that didn't already exist. They change the trajectory of something.

This book is not about innovation per se, but a side note here about my thinking on innovation. Innovation can involve creating something completely out of thin air, but frequently it can involve improving on something that existed before or bringing together previously separate approaches or concepts to create a new way. I'll use concepts I call "transformational innovation" and "incremental innovation." Transformational innovation is creation where there is no reversing it, like creating a chemical compound. Incremental innovation brings together pieces to improve on something.

An example to illuminate what I mean by innovation as the "creation of the new" is in the field of music composition. If you are familiar with the history of Western music, you'll know that through most of early Western history, music was "monophonic"—that is, one single melody line performed at a time. Though simplistic, this music could be beautiful, moving, and clean. In the latter part of the Middle Ages, musical composition took a dramatic turn when composers began to take multiple separate (monophonic) musical lines and combine them to be delivered simultaneously in one piece of music, thus creating "polyphony." From that point Western music was transformed forever, with composers creating more complexity with additional lines, voices, and instruments coming together at the same time to create nuanced, intricate music. This is creation of the "new."

Yet in my definition, for innovation to be relevant, it has to create something that is not only "new" but is "needed." An innovation is relevant when it advances humanity in some way, whether individuals, organizations, or society as a whole. Sometimes the "needed" means helping people come to know that they needed something, even if they didn't know it before—helping them conceive of a brighter future in light of the innovation. Leaders who are innovative welcome uncertainty and, in fact, see possibility in uncertainty. They create innovations that are needed in that possibility; in other words, they create value for society.

So a key characteristic of the innovative business leader is he generates new and needed approaches, methodologies, and tools.

For example, several years ago a concept called "mobile money" was devised and piloted in several developing countries. Mobile money has since gone on to be scaled up in multiple countries so far and has completely transformed how people in those countries do banking. Mobile money brought together the factors of a proliferation of basic mobile phones and cheap airtime in the face of inadequate and unreliable banking infrastructure and rural populations without easy access to brick and mortar banking facilities. Once broadly adopted, mobile money facilitated conversion of economies that were essentially cash economies to modern electronic means for transacting business and moving money.

An innovator also creates and promulgates novel designs and solutions that advance a specific professional field. Steve Jobs—though there were many other parts of his leadership that were not laudable—was, of course, an innovator. At least in the tech world, he was arguably the greatest innovator of our time, dramatically advancing the field of information technology.

Jobs envisioned a world where people everywhere were connected to computing devices and connected to the world all the time, regardless of where they were. He saw linkages and possibilities that virtually no one else in the world saw—or if they did, they didn't have the will to act on it. He advanced the field of consumer technology in ways that people will study and model one hundred years from now. I will not spend more time on Jobs here since so much has been written about him, other than to say he embodied what I mean by a business leader who is also a thought leader and innovator.

Another example comes from my experience in the government contracting industry. In the '60s and '70s as the government contracting business was expanding substantially, competition was increasing and the process for pursuing and winning large government contracts was becoming hugely expensive, time consuming, and laborious. With the highly rigorous and regulated way in which business had to be pursued, proposals prepared and won, only a few organizations had the bandwidth to compete. Proposals to federal government clients were required to be extremely detailed and highly technical (e.g., how to design and assemble a fighter jet), yet engineers and analysts were basically terrible at marketing and sales.

Enter Steve Shipley. Shipley decided that if he and his associates could develop, document, and teach a standard way for technical people to capture and win government business, they could even the playing field. The Shipley approach quickly gained traction such that by the 1990s, almost every government contracting firm was applying some form of Shipley's methodologies. Shipley Associates even founded an association called the Association of Proposal Management Professionals. Forty years and many innovation cycles later, the Shipley way is still the gold standard. This innovative solution advanced the field of business development, it was both new *and* needed, and it permanently changed the trajectory of government contracting. See www.shipleywins. com for more information.

Another characteristic of innovation is that the thought leader's inputs carry the weight of evidence—just the fact that an idea came from that thought leader immediately gives it credibility. In other words, for the thought leader, the fact that it was their idea or just their endorsement of an idea creates citable evidence that confirms the validity of that idea.

Farley Cleghorn's word carries the weight of evidence. During my time at Futures Group, we were starting to get some feedback from clients that the technical innovations and ideas described in our proposals were becoming stale and were not as compelling as they had previously been. When Farley became chief technical officer at Futures Group, one of the things we agreed on was that he would ensure we changed the market perception that we were becoming stale. We set up a structure that all technical proposals had to have his stamp of approval before they could leave the confines of Futures Group and go to a client.

On the occasions when I would get involved in aspects of proposals, sometimes staff would ask me if I were OK with them sending the proposal out. My first question was, "Has Farley approved the technical approach?" I am not convinced that Farley actually read every word of every technical proposal—though, knowing him, he might have—but his word alone carried the weight of evidence. If he said it was OK, then it was OK.

Others I have mentioned in this chapter also have that phenomenon, such as John Stover, the world-renowned modeler and forecaster. John's work had become so proven and trusted over the years that all he had to do was put his name behind an idea and people took it as truth.

An innovator also sees and leverages linkages across disciplines. An example of this characteristic is Rich Podurgal. I mentioned him in Chapter 1 on *Individual Wisdom*. At Constella Group, we hired Rich to join us as the executive head of our human resources function at a critical juncture in our company's evolution. To signify where we were headed with that function, we renamed it "Organization and People Development" rather than human resources.

Rich came to our company having been a senior human resources executive at GlaxoSmithKline (GSK), one of the world's leading pharmaceutical companies. At GSK, Rich had worked with and helped develop some of the world's best leaders in the pharma industry. He came to our small but thriving company and rocked our world. I could probably write multiple chapters about the transformation Rich helped bring to Constella (maybe that will be another book), but for now, I'll highlight a specific innovation Rich brought to us that demonstrates this characteristic.

Partway into his tenure at Constella, and as we were growing dramatically, Rich designed an internal leadership development program for us. Called LEAD (Leading with Excellence, Action, and Dialogue), the program was a yearlong intensive on-the-job leadership development endeavor designed to transform both the current and next generation of leaders. LEAD had a combination of didactic training, outside coursework, and on-the-job mentoring and coaching; it culminated in a group project to address a real business need. We ran cohorts of leaders from diverse disciplines through the program in staggered six-month increments so we would have two to three cohorts running at any one time. LEAD had a mix of practical and theoretical, and individual and group work.

Importantly, Rich first gained full buy-in from our founder and other executive leaders like me because he knew this could not just be an HR training project on the side. For this initiative to really make an impact, it had to be mainstreamed into the day-to-day life of our company and its executive leaders. LEAD was innovation—the creation of the new and the needed. I am sure Rich pulled from best practice and his own experience at GSK, but for us at Constella, this was transformational.

At the time we sold our company, Constella Group, to a $2 billion public company, our people development and leadership culture was like nothing our buyer had itself or had ever seen. Our people leadership approaches were more mature than a company ten times our size. More important, people initiatives like LEAD and others created tangible business value in helping Constella obtain the maximum valuation for our company when we did sell. So Rich Podurgal turned out to be a thought leader in leadership itself.

ACTIVE INTERNALLY. In my definition, true thought leaders are not only active externally but are also active internally—that is, focused inward and helping attract, develop, and inspire others in their field. The behaviors exhibited internally by thought leaders include being a mentor to others, being a magnet for attracting talent, inspiring others to achieve, and helping others get ideas into the marketplace. These behaviors interconnect to each other and to other behaviors I describe in *Individual Wisdom*, so below I will highlight them all together.

My statistician friend Rich Cohn, from Constella Group days, engendered such loyalty in his people that through multiple rounds of his group being bought and sold, he managed to hold them together. I think his teams would have followed him anywhere.

Rich would not describe himself as the nationally respected PhD statistician that he is, focused on researching the effects of the environment on health, but he would beam at being described as a *mentor* to others. Rich not only was a *magnet* for attracting key talent but he developed and retained that talent. He *inspired* highly technical people to greatness. He mentored them and convinced them to do things they never thought they could or would do. For example, most of the technical researchers he hired never imagined participating in dreaded business development. Over time, Rich helped his teams see why they should participate in business development efforts and why, in fact, they were the best suited to do so.

John Stover, mentioned earlier, was also an active mentor internally. He was so unassuming he could have been the pleasant, quiet analyst occupying the cube down the hall from you. But John was legendary internally. As I noted above, John left Futures Group soon after I got involved with the organization, but I quickly heard from numerous mid-level staff how our company would never be the same and their careers would never be the same without John there to continue mentoring them. Even other senior technical folks who were already becoming well published and presenting externally wanted John's advice, support, and approval.

So after John left to start his own company, Futures Group established a close working relationship with him such that he could continue to be a mentoring resource for our own staff. One of the things that made John a great mentor internally to other aspiring staff was that he was generous with his time and ideas. This applies to other thought leaders I mentioned above as well. A common thread is the willingness to give time and authentic interest in helping others advance (see Chapter 2, *Individual Wisdom*).

I mentioned earlier that one of my great mentors was David Walker, the CFO for a time at BDM, my first company. In three years of working for him, and having come into that role literally without one minute of financial or accounting training, I felt like I received an on-the-job MBA and probably even could have sat for the CPA exam (God forbid).

He mentored me intensely. He annoyed me and drove me crazy sometimes, but he saw things in me that I didn't even see in myself. He worked on teaching me things on days when I didn't want to learn and shoved me ahead at times when I just wanted to go back to doing chi-squared tests or running regression analyses. But I did learn and grow. I credit David today for having given me that MBA, for giving me a foundation that allowed me to be successful in growing toward being a Complete Business Leader.

His leadership style back then was brusque and direct, but he made me better—way better. Ultimately, I had to be open to receive that mentoring, but David struck a fine balance of motivating me without pushing me so hard that I rejected him.

I knew I had arrived in David's eyes several years later after I had left the corporate finance group and moved back into my company's technical, revenue-producing side of the business. When David had some new corporate financial issues and challenges and was trying to figure out how to incorporate changes into the business's operations, he sought me out. He asked me for help.

And then when our company, BDM, made its first foray into international mergers and acquisitions (M&A) by buying a company in Germany, he recommended me to help lead an integration effort. He wanted me on the team because I understood both corporate finance and the projects side of the business. And I could translate what needed to happen to the German corporate functions and project management teams in ways that would be respected and understood.

Years later at a different company, David was awarded CFO of the Year by two different industry associations in our government contracting industry (so he was recognized externally as well), but I never forgot his willingness to invest in and mentor me.

One of the hallmarks of a thought leader is they are well past making it all about themselves (except perhaps people like Steve Jobs). Rather, they make it about others. People like Rich Cohn and John Stover saw their role as helping other professionals get ideas out into the marketplace. One of the key components of this success in technical fields I have worked in is helping someone else get their research peer-reviewed and published. Often, you'll see senior technical experts working with more junior professionals on a journal article but insisting that their names be first in the author list. I witnessed both Rich and John purposely put their names later in the listing to give junior and mid-level staff more of the limelight in publishing.

I am a singer. It is a side hobby for me. Actually, it's well beyond a hobby; singing one of my life's great passions. I am a pretty good tenor, though never good enough to make a career of it. If I were, I probably wouldn't be writing books on business leadership.

Rodney Wynkoop was the longtime director of choral activities at Duke University and is also director of the Choral Society of Durham. I sang under Rodney for about fifteen years. Rodney is a thought leader in choral conducting. He is well known regionally and nationally. He has perfect pitch—as a singer, it's pretty scary when your director has perfect pitch. He can pick out a mistake or slight intonation issue from one singer in a group of 150. Rodney is exacting and demanding of singers who sing under his baton. Though he is warm and soft spoken outside of a choral setting, he can be tough and unrelenting during rehearsals and performances in a quest for creating perfect music. The Choral Society of Durham is an all-volunteer singing group, so we volunteer to be part of that unrelenting quest.

Rodney is a magnet for attracting talented singers to sing for him. Thought leaders must be a *magnet for talent*. Over the years, Rodney Wynkoop has been able to attract a level of volunteer singing talent that is unmatched anywhere else in the region: people like me who work a day job all day and sing at night, or other choral directors and musicians who just love to sing choral music with Rodney because of the caliber of music we produce, or soloists (albeit paid) who choose to perform concerts with our group because of Rodney.

Rodney also inspires. Thought leaders must *inspire others*. Rodney brings us individually and collectively as a group of 150 singers to new heights in choral music. He inspires us to be better than we are or thought we could be. He calls— no, commands—us to be absolutely the best. I suppose that would not be inspiring for some casual singers, but for those of us who deeply love singing, it is inspirational to work so hard together to create the highest form of art we can. We don't want to disappoint him. We don't want to disappoint each other and, more important, we don't want to disappoint ourselves individually.

I remember for the first couple of years I sang with Rodney and the Choral Society of Durham, I was intimidated—not my natural state as an executive business leader. I didn't think Rodney even knew who I was or really knew my voice. Then one night after a rehearsal, he stopped me out of the blue and called me by name (I didn't know he even knew my name). He said, "Chris, I just wanted to tell you how much I like your voice and how happy I am to have you singing with us. You really sounded great tonight." Wow, I was soaring after that! I was totally inspired to work even harder to make music beyond my abilities.

SUMMARY COMMENTS

Let me make one final note here of what thought leadership is NOT. In my years since the early '90s, while involved in the public health, life sciences, and health care markets, I have seen many organizations—usually large ones trying to break into the health field from some other adjacent domain—hire their "token doctor." These are organizations that somehow

THE COMPLETE BUSINESS LEADER

thought they could hire one senior person with the medical doctor letters after their name and automatically be credible in the field of health. That medical doctor usually gets a fancy title, like chief medical officer. That person may be quite competent generally, but a big title and letters after someone's name do not mean they are a thought leader. And it certainly does not imbue thought leadership on the organization writ large.

I have laid out three primary competencies of how I define a thought leader in the context of Complete Business Leaders: active externally, an innovator, and active internally. Each of these has several example behaviors that I have described. I have also made the case that in today's global knowledge economy, it is not enough for a business leader to learn and apply general management principles. A complete leader must include being a thought leader—a recognized expert in something.

Most of the leaders I cited above to demonstrate a specific characteristic of *Thought Leadership* actually could have been cited under numerous other characteristics. Such is the nature of the Complete Business Leadership framework. The seven dimensions are interconnected.

Over my own career, I have resisted the temptation to pigeonhole myself or stay in one lane for a long, long time. I described how I was on the path to becoming a thought leader in clinical data management but jumped off that before I arrived. So, then, in what area am I a thought leader? I have known and highlighted many thought leaders for whom I have deep affection and respect. I also I felt like I had to study myself as one of the subjects in the Complete Business Leader framework to confirm the model. If I couldn't realistically assess my own qualifications as a thought leader, then I couldn't very well defend this component of the CBL framework.

So there are two areas where I believe I meet those characteristics I laid out. Neither is actually a traditional "technical" skill, though I am quite comfortable and reasonably well known in the health IT sector as a technical discipline.

The first is in the business aspects of government contracting. I have spent the better part of my career in that trade, I have become recognized externally, I have been a speaker and writer on the topic, I have mentored others, and I have brought innovations to organizations in the business of government contracting. I am quite comfortable in this subject area, and I could go toe to toe with anyone in the business of government contracting.

The second is in leadership. In my case, I have made a thirty-year study of it. Since my first role in my first company, I have watched, learned, and applied business leadership principles. I have grown and expanded; I have been coached, mentored, evaluated, and tested. I have now spoken externally, mentored internally, and created the framework we are discussing today. Have I arrived? No. As I mentioned earlier, once you think you have arrived, then you are automatically disqualified to be a Complete Business Leader. I have much more to learn and many more ways to grow.

By the end of *The Wizard of Oz* movie, the Scarecrow was a thought leader. He had intimate knowledge of the forest, the witch, and her castle and had a deep understanding of the strengths and weaknesses of his traveling colleagues. The witch knew she needed to go after the Scarecrow first when the group of travelers was attacked, which means he was recognized externally. As a thought leader, he mentored the others and had become the de facto inspirational leader of the group. And he constantly innovated throughout the journey, coming up with new ways to achieve their mission and to save Dorothy and others. And he didn't even need a diploma or a fancy title—like chief innovation officer—to be a thought leader.

Some people without brains do an awful lot of talking, don't they?
—Scarecrow, *The Wizard of Oz movie*

Competency	Example Behavior
Active externally	o Proactively and consistently publishes o Is recognized by peers and called upon frequently as a speaker/presenter and advisor o Serves in leadership in professional societies, committees, and workgroups o Is external to the company—excites the market and professional community
Innovator	o Generates "new" and "needed" approaches, methodologies, and tools o Creates and promulgates innovative solution design and problem-solving that advances the field o Offers inputs that carry the weight of evidence o Sees and leverages linkages across disciplines
Active internally	o Serves as a mentor to other professional staff o Is a magnet for attracting professional talent o Inspires colleagues o Is able and willing to help others promote and publish ideas

BUSINESS GROWTH

Without continual growth and progress, such words as
improvement, achievement, and success have no meaning.
—Benjamin Franklin

The lifeblood of a professional services business is business growth. There is no such thing as inventory or monthly ordering patterns from consumers. There are no factories or equipment that can be repurposed or sold off. You either win more projects, which allows you to hire more talented people, which begets more projects, or your competition is winning those projects and then taking all *your* good people, which means you are then shrinking since revenue and profit generation is highly correlated with how many people you have. You must have talented people to win in a services business. My first manager, Frank, introduced me to the concept that "If you are not growing, you're shrinking."

When I was twenty-two, I got my first taste of business development blood. I was working on a project—a pretty small task order, actually. My manager, Frank, had described the "triple threat" concept to me that I referred to in the Introduction (one who can win business, manage projects, and manage people), and he explained to me that the quickest way to get ahead in our company was to grow the business. He also introduced me to a concept referred to as "Eat what you kill," which meant if I won some business, then I could manage it, hire people to work it, and expand my little empire.

So I came up with an idea for some add-on work (some might call this "upselling") to what I was already doing on my existing task order. I wrote a concept paper, scoped out the idea, and pitched it to the client. After a few meetings, the client decided he liked the idea and went searching for additional funding. After a few more meetings and tweaking the scope and budget, the client found the money and managed to work it through all the contracting paperwork, adding about $50,000 to our small task order. I was ecstatic! What a feeling that was.

Of course, the $50,000 seems so small now, but at the time, that was my first taste of business development blood. And I liked the taste; I was hooked. I didn't know what the hell I was doing or how I had done it, but wow—it felt great.

A Complete Business Leader ideally should be a hunter and should love to chase and win business. Or if not naturally a hunter, the Complete Business Leader must learn to hunt some and then be able to identify and attract other hunters to pick up the spear. The Complete Business Leader must be hardwired toward growth. It must be etched into their DNA, like breathing.

This chapter is about growing the business. It is geared to a professional services business because that's what

I know best. I have divided it into three main sections: opportunity development, capture management, and proposal development. These three sections are generally sequential, from creating or identifying an unmet need (opportunity development) to putting together a strategy or solution to meet that need (capture management) to conveying it in a written sales document that results in the award of a contract (proposal management).

Some of what you'll hear in this chapter is, for sure, unique to the kinds of large-scale professional services and business outsourcing projects I have been involved with most for my career, but I think some of the competencies are applicable in much broader contexts.

One other adjacent topic I'll address briefly at the end of this chapter is business growth through acquisition. Mergers and acquisitions (M&A) growth actually has many of the same characteristics as hunting for organic growth, including the systematic rigor required. More on that later.

One of the things I learned along the way is that business development, while a hunter's game, requires a systematic, disciplined, repeatable approach to be consistently successful. Just ask a hunter. A novice might walk into a forest and, practically at random, find a deer and manage to take it down. But that same novice could walk into that same forest one hundred more times and never even see a deer, much less manage to shoot and kill it.

To be consistently good at hunting, the hunter must have a process, practice that process, follow that process religiously, and then exhibit flexibility and resilience to overcome unexpected obstacles (say, bad weather) to consistently come home with game. The hunter must study where the targets typically show up and at what time of day they are most likely to show, and even the time of year. The hunter must practice over and over how to hit and take down the target on the first shot and must practice the patience required to wait, wait, wait for the right moment. Fire too soon and the target bolts away unharmed. Fire too late and another hunter has taken the shot or the target moves behind a tree.

(For full disclosure, I hate hunting as a sport. I went hunting when I was a kid, shot one rabbit, watched it bleed to death, and was cured immediately of any desire that I wanted to shoot and kill animals. Hunting new projects and defeating competitors in that hunt . . . now *that* I am ok with!)

So what you will see in the sections below is a set of disciplines that I have found are necessary to predictably pursue and win professional services business. These disciplines, practiced and followed systematically and combined with a thirst for business development (BD) blood, will result in business growth success.

By the way, having a systematic process by itself is not sufficient. You can be a slave to the process and not be consistently successful.

For example, in the early 1990s at my company, BDM, I was trying to grow a new consulting practice with the US Food and Drug Administration (FDA) as our client. The FDA was outsourcing an increasing amount of work to contractors. FDA needed substantial help with its overall IT systems and how it managed its information. FDA had (still does have) massive data and document needs and was drowning in disparate data, documents, and databases. FDA was my client account and one of my key clients. I was leading all BDM's efforts with FDA to manage current projects and grow new projects. There was a large procurement we knew was coming. The project would be highly competitive, and we were positioning to win.

My firm had recently established a corporate function specifically to manage the systematic process of new business pursuit. I engaged that group as a support function to help me win that bid. We religiously followed the state-of-the-art methods and made use of all the associated tools. We followed the process to the letter. And we lost.

About a year later, there was another large FDA procurement coming, and I convinced a senior executive within the firm named Bill McQuiggan to help me win. Bill believed in and followed a systematic process but had a track record of overlaying that process with other intangibles. Bill was a Zen master of BD, almost legendary—not just within our company but across our whole industry (see Chapter 4, *Thought Leadership*: Bill was considered a thought leader in business development). He had an intangible sense of just what was needed at each part of the business development cycle.

Bill willingly jumped in as a favor to me. Bill drove the overall capture and proposal process with me working alongside him. Bill let me in on one of his winning techniques: He followed the structured capture and proposal processes (described later in this chapter), allowing teams of people to be involved and shape the proposal with all their strategic ideas, solution designs, inputs and early proposal drafts, except for the executive summary of the proposal, which he wrote himself early in the process. Then toward the end of the proposal process, Bill took the entire boring, rough draft one-hundred-page proposal, thanked all the proposal contributors for their work, and locked himself away for five to six days. When he returned, he brought back a beautiful, compelling proposal draft ready for final editing.

Bill believed that the written proposal had to read more like a personal letter directly to the reader (the proposal evaluators on the client side). When Bill had finished, the proposal read like a single person wrote it, had compelling win themes woven throughout the document, and held together as a single narrative on why our company should be selected for the bid. And we won! By watching him, I learned an immense amount about how to balance rigorous process with an unyielding commitment to win. I have never forgotten that lesson from Bill. And through that experience, I had my own mini experiment of what it takes to win. The lesson I learned is to follow the process but don't be a slave to process over substance.

Throughout this chapter, I will refer to various pivotal big wins I have been involved in, and frequently I'll refer to a program called VAERS (the Vaccine Adverse Event Reporting System) that I led a team to win initially in 2001. VAERS was a big government outsourcing program overseen by the Centers for Disease Control and Prevention (CDC) that involves managing a national database of vaccine adverse events reported by the public and health care providers. VAERS included public reporting, database management, and analytics around the data to be shared with researchers. The program also included a hotline that the public could use if they had questions or concerns about vaccines. I'll use VAERS as an example throughout because it exhibits many of the steps and competencies of business development.

I personally led that win. Since that win in 2001, I have led or been involved with numerous other much larger and just as competitive wins, but VAERS still sticks out in my memory because of its transformational elements for me and for Constella Group.

When we chased and won VAERS, I had not been at Constella Group long. We were still a small company with $15 million in revenue. By the time I arrived at Constella at the end of 1998, I had already uncovered my innate thirst for BD blood and had learned the disciplined steps of successful business growth at my previous large company, BDM. So when I joined Constella, I was able to bring all that learning to bear. As I noted earlier, Constella's culture was welcoming of new learning and ideas from outside the company.

My boss, Don Holzworth, was also a hunter, and he was very clear from the beginning that he had hired me to grow the business. So I pursued and led the win of VAERS, following what I had learned from Bill McQuiggan.

VAERS was outsourced by CDC to a contractor and was coming up for contract competition again the next year. Once I arrived at Constella and saw the corporate capabilities I had to work with, I felt like we could get positioned to win VAERS. Over a twelve-month period, I met with CDC and other colleagues, performed research, and explored new approaches. When the actual proposal time came, we had done so much background and positioning work that it was all over but the celebrating—I can say that in retrospect now, but of course at the time it was not a sure thing that we would win.

But then it was competitive. In government contracting, the proposal evaluation process is so rigorous that no matter how much great positioning work you did before, if you don't convey that in the written proposal, you'll lose.

So, for thirty days during the proposal preparation time, a team of writers and I worked sixteen to eighteen hours a day. Though a team worked on it, I ended up personally writing or rewriting most of the fifty-page proposal. My boss, Don, was a master of pricing, among many things. He and I sat together at his kitchen table for hours on multiple nights, working on pricing to be as innovative and price sensitive as possible without sacrificing our ability to actually execute it if we won.

In the months after we submitted our proposal, I fretted and sweated. I continued to do research and follow-up as much as was legal. And then the email came that we had won. I went running down the hall to Don's office, and he actually hugged me! Kindred spirits in the hunt.

As I noted, winning that proposal was transformational for Constella and for me. For one thing, it was one of the first "full and open" competitions Constella had won. As a small business up to that point, Constella mostly won contracts that were set aside for only small businesses to compete on. Second, VAERS was important, meaningful public health work that fit our mission and aligned well with our value proposition. Our proposed solutions were, at the time, groundbreaking: sharing information with clients and researchers all online through a virtual private network, online web reporting and database access, and new approaches to toll-free hotlines. Finally, the win was transformational for Constella because we documented the capture management approach I had applied, and from then on it became the company's way of winning business.

For me, it proved my value to Constella and set me down a course to eventually run most of the company. I was very thirsty when I came to Constella and chased the VAERS contract like it was an oasis in the desert.

To this day that VAERS win is one of my career mountaintop moments.

COMPETENCIES OF BUSINESS GROWTH

As noted earlier, I have divided the phases of *Business Growth* into three major competency areas, each of which requires a set of activities and behaviors.

OPPORTUNITY DEVELOPMENT. The first major phase of *Business Growth* is identifying and developing new business opportunities. Some of this is intuition, some is the will and intentionality, and some is disciplined process.

A Complete Business Leader creates or identifies opportunities by engaging clients and partners in genuine conversation. It's not a sales conversation; rather, it's listening and learning what is missing or what is needed. The leader then begins to form innovative ideas to address what is missing. That could be a new solution or a repackaging of existing products or offerings. And being authentic with a potential client may mean recommending things you can't offer them but someone else can. These conversations are the start of the value creation chain: recognizing an unmet need or desire and exploring a world of possible ideas to meet that unmet need or desire.

To create or identify these opportunities for new value creation, the Complete Business Leader must hone the skills we discussed in earlier chapters of being curious, intuitive, and perceptive; actively listening; and authentically wanting value to be delivered to the potential client. This is not selling. What it does involve, though, is conveying credibility with potential clients and partners.

In my experience, every client, every deal or new project, is distinct. But a common thread in each instance is that you have to be able to convey *not* that you have all the answers but that you have the right questions. This conveys a credibility with clients that you can work to solve their problems and create value for them—that they can trust you.

Richard Branson, founder and chairman of the Virgin Group conglomerate of businesses, is legendary for his rabid focus on listening to the market and potential clients, figuring out what is missing, and then creating a new approach or product that will delight the market. From his start launching a mail-order record business in the early 1970s to launching Virgin airlines, he had a keen ear to hear what people wanted and an eye for what was possible. For example, in the airline industry, Branson saw an opening to treat flyers to a fun flying experience that made passengers feel special, like they were all in first class, at an affordable price.[14]

Another required set of behaviors for opportunity development is discipline and rigor. This means systematically following up, documenting conversations, conducting research, and seeking outside inputs. This is not the sexy part of the hunting. Discipline and rigor are necessary behaviors of a good, consistently successful hunter. If the hunter is inconsistent and sloppy in his preparations, his family or tribe might have lots to eat for a few days but then starve to death in the weeks following.

I'll share an example of the research and rigor required. In 2005, we learned of a large potential new project being crafted by one of Constella's major clients called the National Institute for Environmental Health Sciences (NIEHS), one of the twenty-seven institutes of the National Institutes of Health. The procurement was still almost a year away. We thought the project, which was to take a more clinical (that is, in humans) research approach to the interactions of the environment on health outcomes, would be quite large and also very impactful to public health. In particular, in the aftermath of the Katrina disaster in New Orleans (August 2005), this research program would explore all of the environmental factors surrounding Katrina and its short and longer-term health effects on populations.

My colleague Rich Cohn began the disciplined process of meeting with multiple officials within NIEHS to both determine whether this would be the type of work we could do and help influence the ideas that would be part of the project's scope. Rich set up a regular schedule of calling on NIEHS officials. He conducted in-depth research on the latest professional discourse in journal articles. He regularly sought the opinions of other experts in the field. He followed the research trail wherever it led.

Along the way, Rich became convinced that, while it would be an uphill battle against renowned research competition (such as RTI International), Constella Group had applicable qualifications and some innovative approaches that would make a difference in the project if and when it were ever released. Rich understood our company's value proposition, he was creating innovative solutions to solve real problems, and he was systematic and disciplined. I'll come back to this clinical research story later.

As a side note, I have immense respect for RTI. In fact, RTI has served as the measuring stick for me for years in health science research. RTI is a sometimes-unruly set of academically oriented researchers, but those experts are some of the best in the world, and they are hard to beat in a competitive procurement when they are able to muster their full focus on something.

Another critical behavior here is persistence. Rich was (and is) a mild-mannered PhD statistician. But he was what I sometimes call "pleasantly persistent." He just kept at things, following the research wherever it led. Rich was not easily stopped. He would run into a roadblock—for example, some other outside researcher who didn't want to share an idea—and he would just find another way to get the information. He didn't pound the table or forcibly get the information he needed; rather, he would just smile and go work around the roadblock or chop through it until he broke through. Rich had a steely determination to get the information he needed.

Another key component in this stage of opportunity development is overlaying a deep understanding of the buying habits, practices, and requirements of the client and the broader marketplace. For example, all the different US government agencies I have worked with fall under common federal procurement regulations, but each agency has its own nuances. It is critical to understand those nuances, even as early as in the opportunity development phase, to help objectively assess whether you can win or get positioned to win.

A final aspect I'll address here goes back to the discipline and rigor. This characteristic in the opportunity development stage includes being able to objectively decide when to stop chasing an opportunity. This is possibly the hardest discipline to hone, particularly for more natural hunters. Natural hunters have to learn to balance the energy and resources required and probability of success versus the payoff of a kill.

For my colleague Rich, this was actually relatively easy because he was such a data-driven researcher, always coming back to the facts at hand. He could pretty objectively determine whether or not an opportunity should be dropped. Sometimes I pushed him to be more aggressive and take chances, but I never doubted his analysis of the situation. For example, when Rich came back to me at some point and said, "I think the NIEHS clinical research project is winnable," I really didn't have to interrogate that further. I just poured more business development resources into his hands to pursue the opportunity.

CAPTURE MANAGEMENT. The second major phase of the business development life cycle is capture management. In my line of work, this is the most intense part and is usually where a project is won or lost. In the opportunity development phase described above, we are qualifying an opportunity to determine *whether we can get positioned to win*. Now in the capture management phase, we are actually doing the things that *will position us to win*.

This stage is less objective and more about doing a bunch of steps right that will lead to winning. With teams I have led, they know what I mean when I say, "We have to now execute all of the 'ninety-six steps' needed to win." This specifically refers to the Shipley method (described later in this chapter and also in Chapter 4, *Thought Leadership*), which lays out a series of detailed steps that, when followed, increase the probability of winning. More generally, I would say that sweating the sometimes boring details and doing all of the little things well does not ensure winning but certainly increases the chances of winning.

One of the key disciplines in capture management is identifying or creating the value distinctions that we can offer—that is, the distinct approaches or solutions our team can offer that create value for the client. While this requires an objective, realistic eye to what is and is not possible, it also requires a level of creativity. We must be realistic about what our current real value proposition is, but the creativity shows up in being able to shape a value proposition that may not exist today.

Creating that value proposition requires a deep understanding of the client's needs and of the current project at hand. It also requires the ability to create innovative, compelling solutions that build on our organization's core strengths and capabilities—to see a possible future that even the client may not have thought of. This creativity might involve combining a set of diverse capabilities and approaches, partners, and tools that have never been put together before but that, when combined, can create something original.

A corollary to the discipline of creating value distinctions is what I sometimes call "changing the playing field." What I mean by this is, if what the client thinks they need doesn't fit your core capabilities but you think you still have value to add to the client, then reshape the client's view. This does *not* mean force fit what you do onto the client; rather, it means reframe what you do in a manner that plays to your strengths AND in a way that delivers value to the client in ways they may not have thought of before

This reframing must be done in a way that is still authentic with the client in mind. In the end, what you are offering must deliver something of value, since clients determine value anyway, or it will not stick.

To use a sports analogy, more and more college football teams have recently discovered that if they don't have the raw talent to compete in a very physical slow-tempo defensive struggle with the likes of powerhouse University of Alabama, they need to change the nature of the game. Many teams have started playing an up-tempo, fast-paced game where they spread out defenses and try to get them tired out. In other words, they are changing the traditional nature of the game rather than playing Alabama's brute force physical brand of football.

This doesn't always work, of course. Alabama still wins about 90 percent of the games it plays, but increasingly teams have had individual game success against Alabama by playing a somewhat different game—changing the playing field.

To bring that concept back to our public health research game, if you compete against RTI head to head, trying to beat them on research prowess alone, you'll lose almost every time. So you have to redefine the game to play to your strengths.

In the NIEHS clinical research example I mentioned above, as part of our capture management process we had to define a value proposition where we, Constella, could win. This involved bringing on other partners to blunt the research advantage RTI had. We also brought on a couple of unconventional partners—ones that would not typically be part of a government-funded research project—to shake things up. Our capture management efforts also involved developing some new research data capture methods that had not been used before. We felt like this would create new value for NIEHS; of course, only NIEHS could ultimately determine whether this was valuable to them. Finally, we felt like we had more practical knowledge than our main competitors; we knew how to turn the research into steps that were actionable (new policies, regulations, public education campaigns, etc.).

This was *changing the playing field.* Our assessment was that RTI would play the game as a traditional research program, whereas we changed the game into applying the research to change practice.

I should note here that, though RTI is the benchmark opponent in health science research, we are not certain that they actually put in a bid against us for this NIEHS project. Early on, we knew that RTI was clearly positioning to bid; however, because of Rich's early, clever, persistent capture activities, including securing a critical partner institution to team with us, other competitors such as RTI may have backed away from even bidding.

Another key piece of effective capture management is integrating technical approaches and solutions with price. For various clients, price may be more or less important, but in my experience, it is never unimportant. In fact, we could argue that creating value *always* has some input cost that should be reflected in the price we are offering to the client. Creating value is never free. So we must be able to strike the balance of creating new approaches and solutions that either (1) fit within a client's budget or (2) match a client's perception of value as determined by the client's willingness to pay a bit more for these approaches and solutions.

Public sector clients I have worked with all have budgets, so the minimum required is to define a set of project solutions that fit within their budget. Commercial clients, in the pharmaceutical industry I have dealt mostly with, may have project budgets; however, in my experience, commercial clients are more apt to make an integrated decision based on weighing the amount of value you can create for the price you are proposing.

Specifically, for the pharmaceutical services industry, Constella Group provided clinical trials outsourcing services. The clinical trials process is highly regulated and takes years to get through. Every day longer in the clinical trial process is one day less of patent protection a pharma company has. So the overriding calculation of a pharma company in the clinical trials process was not how much it would cost to run the trial but whether our approach (even if a bit more expensive) could get them to FDA approval a day quicker. Large new "blockbuster" drugs are still generally measured with a heuristic of $1 million in sales per day. Every day saved in the clinical trials timeline creates $1 million in sales to the pharma company, and every day delayed in approval costs them $1 million in sales.

Part of the art and discipline of the capture management cycle is weighing the cost and value creation potential of our strategies, and most important, understanding how the client will weigh that formula.

A final discipline of the capture management phase is putting together winning teams. This includes project teams with outside partners, if needed, to create value, as well as the individual people that will form the project team. In my line of work, coming up with a project team is a critical scored component of what the client will value and how they will make a competitive selection. For example, selecting the right people for project director or technical leaders of your proposed solution can signal to your client whether you really understand their needs.

Back to my NIEHS example: After objectively weighing various alternatives, we collectively determined that bidding my colleague Rich (the PhD statistician) as the overall project director/principal investigator would yield the best chance of winning. Rich had no pride around this. If we had determined that someone else would be a better fit for the client's needs, Rich would have been fine with not being proposed as the project director. Rich just wanted to win, in his pleasantly persistent way. In the end, you know you created the right mix of project team and external teammates when the client validates your team by selecting you over others.

As described above here, there are a host of specific disciplines and steps that must be honed in the capture management phase. Across all of those steps in getting positioned to win, you must:

- o Know your client: what they value and how they buy—and then develop a solution that creates value for them.
- o Know your competition: their strengths, weaknesses, and tendencies—and develop a set of solutions that level the playing field or shift it away from favoring the competition.
- o Know yourself: your strengths, weaknesses, and tendencies—and leverage this knowledge to put yourself into the best position to win.

PROPOSAL DEVELOPMENT. The final phase of the business development cycle is preparing a winning proposal. There are a range of specific activities and disciplines involved in this phase.

In some industries, preparing the written proposal is just the final stage of the sales process and might largely be boilerplate—standard company platitudes and a price quote. However, in the government contracting world, the written proposal is usually required to be detailed and compelling, tailored specifically to the individual project requirements, and rigorously scored by a team of evaluators. Actual award of a new project depends significantly on what is in the written document. You can do every one of the earlier steps and stages well, but if you don't create a compelling, high-scoring written proposal, you won't win. Some government bids I have been involved in required only an oral presentation, but even then the presentation was rigorously evaluated and scored, so the same preparation requirements applied.

So how do we get, say, a computer engineer, who might be a great engineer but not particularly liberal artsy (in other words, they may be poor at writing or presenting a compelling story), to write winning proposals?

As I mentioned in the CBL *Thought Leadership* chapter, about forty years ago a firm called Shipley Associates tried to address this issue by creating a highly structured method of having technical people convey compelling approaches, features, and benefits in a way that could be turned into effective prose and graphics. Over the years, the Shipley method has become the de facto standard in US government contracting for preparing proposals, with the premise that using this method on all new business opportunities would, over time, drive up win rates. This claim has been backed up by evidence across multiple companies and market sectors. Many firms worldwide have now adopted elements or hybrid approaches of the Shipley method, including organizations in many other industries beyond US government contracting.

I had the opportunity to learn the Shipley method for capture management and proposal development in the early

1990s through two weeks of intensive training, and I fully bought in. I then had many opportunities in the '90s to apply the Shipley approaches in the real world.

When I moved to the small company Constella Group, I created a slimmed-down version of Shipley and began to get other adopters there. As I moved into broader leadership roles, I made our "skinny" Shipley (a simplified version of the full Shipley method) our standard approach for capture management and proposal development. And then with Futures Group, despite some early resistance, we began to deploy a skinny Shipley approach.

There is no need for me to describe the Shipley method in detail here. If you are interested in learning more, you can find Shipley's website at www.shipleywins.com. What I'll describe a bit more below are the kinds of professional behaviors (that are mostly teachable) that people need in order to apply the Shipley method—or any other new business approach—more effectively.

To have a winning proposal, you must be able to integrate your understanding, technical approach, management approaches, personnel, and corporate experience into a cohesive, compelling story. Part of that story needs to effectively articulate features of your approach and the benefit (to the client) those features create.

Converting winning themes that might have been developed during the capture management stage into well-articulated features that discriminate us from the competition is part science and part art. The art form includes creating an emotional conviction (or even changing an evaluator's mind) within the evaluator panel that selecting our team and approach is best. Evaluators are human, and decisions to select a firm to outsource a project to almost always involve at least some level of subjectivity.

The Shipley method calls for creating storyboards, much like what the advertising and film industry does. This does *not* involve writing proposal text; rather, it involves physically laying out the pages of the proposal, including key themes and graphics—in short, mapping out the whole proposal in a structured way. From this storyboard, even engineers and scientists who are not strong writers are able to write structured proposals that will convey in a compelling way why their firm should be selected.

In my experience, people tend to resist this storyboarding stage. The storyboarding process sometimes feels slow, tedious, and unnatural. People have an idea and they want to immediately get to writing. But once they see how the discipline of the storyboarding makes the later proposal writing part much easier, it all makes sense.

An important component of the storyboard and eventually the proposal is defining key features of your proposed approach and what the benefit is to the client. I call those *feature-benefit* pairs. A feature, such as a new tool for collecting data through a mobile device, must have a benefit to the client or it is irrelevant. The benefit to the client, in this case, might be more reliable data, or quicker access to data, or more data points from a broader population set.

It is usually pretty easy to get people to come up with the features of their approach. People like talking about their new ideas. What is really hard, though, is getting people to determine the benefits of that approach to the client. In fact, in my experience, many people just don't get this. I believe the key to getting it—understanding the benefit derived from a feature—is practicing *empathy*.

Empathy, to me, is simply being able to transport yourself to stand in someone else's shoes—to see the world through their eyes. This empathy is at the core of preparing a winning proposal. So a Complete Business Leader must learn to be empathetic.

Some may say empathy can't be taught. I'll just say that in my experience, you can practice the discipline of imagining the world from someone else's vantage point. Some people seem to be more naturally inclined to be empathetic than others. Maybe this comes from their upbringing or other societal factors. But I think no matter what your natural inclination, you can practice and get better at empathy by asking yourself in every situation, every day:

o   What is the human being over there experiencing right now?
o   What is important to them and why?
o   What are their needs and desires?

Being empathetic makes you a better proposal writer who wins more often, because it is human beings who evaluate proposals and human beings who are buying whatever we are selling.

This practice of empathy even makes us better able to communicate overall themes of our proposal, what makes our approaches better (feature), and why the client should care (benefit). And if we are empathetic, we will convey our proposal in ways that people can get. This also means understanding that some human beings are more linear in their thinking, some are spatially or graphically oriented, some are macro thinkers, and others detail oriented. This is why proposal messages need to be in a combination of prose, graphical representations, and tabular lists. My executive coach, Jane, used to call this "speaking into the listening." In other words, stepping into the reader's shoes and seeing the world from their perspective.

The final behavior I'll address in the proposal development phase is thriving on high intensity, deadline-driven environments. Throughout the opportunity development and capture management phases of the business development life cycle described earlier in this chapter, I have pounded on the point that disciplined process and rigorous systematic preparation are critical. Then in the final proposal development phase of the business development hunt, things begin to move very fast and become extremely intense.

Like the lion that has been stalking, watching, waiting, lying low in the grass, when the moment comes the lion must spring into action with tremendous intensity. It's a deadline-driven environment because if she doesn't get to her prey in time, the moment is lost and she and her cubs go hungry for another day.

Some thrive on these high-intensity settings while others don't, but Complete Business Leaders must be able to function at a high level during these times to be successful, even if they don't like those intense times. Back to my premise of being disciplined and rigorous in preparation, even leaders who don't like these high-pressure environments can function well if they feel prepared and ready. Any successful athlete will tell you that they perform better in a crunch (late in the game when time is running out and they must do something exceptional to win) if they have practiced for those moments over and over.

Whether you are familiar with the Shipley method or not, you'll see a common theme here across this chapter—

that of systematic, disciplined approaches. The larger-than-life salesperson is great, but in highly technical fields with intense competition, even great sales instincts require discipline and rigor to win consistently.

STRATEGIC BUSINESS GROWTH THROUGH M&A

What I have described in this chapter is geared toward organic growth. Yet one further insight to share here is that many of the broad ideas and themes of organic growth also apply to growth through mergers and aquisitions (M&A), so I'll briefly address it here.

Successful M&A requires a disciplined approach if it is going to be an integral part of a business's growth strategy and not just a one-time, one-off experience. It involves systematically identifying and vetting a long pipeline of potential M&A targets (similar to opportunity development), honing that down to a smaller list, and then running activities akin to capture management above. And then once you get to a term sheet, the intensity of due diligence, detailed legal document preparation and negotiation, and ultimately closing the deal feels a lot like the proposal development stage.

It also helps to have that thirst for blood and to experience a rush in the hunt for M&A deals. But this is not a sufficient condition to regularly grow through M&A. What is also needed is that systematic process and discipline.

Toward the end of our Constella Group days before we sold the company, we sold a minority stake in the company to a private equity firm. Inviting private equity into your company is not everyone's cup of tea, but I found, on the whole, they taught us a level of discipline and rigor around M&A that I still apply today. The private equity firm made us better. They worked with us on deals, asked us hard questions, and forced us to do rigorous analysis on valuation, client concentration, management maturity, and strategic fit. Our private equity partners also taught us the discipline of walking away from a deal if necessary.

Back to the lion example: It's sort of like the lion who waits, prepares, watches, and sometimes must walk away from a potential kill. Maybe the prey is too far away (which means the cost in energy required for the lion will be too high to pursue compared to the reward) or the prey has others nearby to protect it. Of course, as the lion and her cubs get hungrier day after day, the lion may get more desperate and take more chances in the hunt. Or sometimes, the lion might let another predator attack first and take down the prey. And then the lion runs off the other predators. In the M&A world, we call this buying a distressed asset!

So, to finish off on this adjacent M&A topic, even if your primary growth strategy is M&A, many of the competencies I discussed above could apply. In fact, each of the seven dimensions of the Complete Business Leader framework could be described in the context of growth through M&A.

An in-depth treatment of M&A would take up an entire book, and I might write that someday to share my practical experiences of what works and doesn't work *after* the deal closes. After being involved in more than a dozen M&A transactions on both the sell and buy side, I have found that no matter what clever finance people calculate in spreadsheets for future cash flows, cost efficiencies, synergies, uses of capital, and the like, management and implementation of the transaction post-close is where *real* value is created or destroyed, not in a spreadsheet.

SUMMARY COMMENTS

As I mentioned at the beginning of this chapter, I am by no means an animal hunter. But I am a business hunter. Even after more than thirty years of doing this work, I still get a rush from the entire new business life cycle. I love the discipline and structure required. I love trying to imagine the client's perspective and what they want. I love figuring out what the competition is doing and why. I love the intensity of the proposal process. There is nothing like the sense of urgency of that final stage to focus the mind and energy. And, finally, I love to win.

Part of becoming a Complete Business Leader is gaining mastery in growing business. Ideally, you would feel the rush from winning new business that many of us do, but even if you don't get the rush, you know that you and your organizational family have to "eat." To eat, you have to hunt. And to hunt reliably, you have to develop some competency at hunting.

I laid out some of the detailed skills needed to effectively grow business, at least in the markets where I have worked. And I grouped these into three phases of a business growth life cycle: opportunity development, capture management, and proposal development. There are a series of specific behaviors and disciplines in each of these phases—skills that can be developed through practice and commitment.

While maybe the hunter instinct can't be trained, many other skills can be. And that leads me back to one of the key themes for successful business growth: being systematic, disciplined, and rigorous in planning and practice.

At the end of the day, Complete Business Leaders must have the overriding commitment to grow their businesses to the benefit of all stakeholders, creating value for clients, employees, partners, and shareholders. And that overriding commitment should drive the Complete Business Leader to learn and apply the systematic, disciplined approaches necessary to grow business.

A lioness can reach top speed of approximately 50 miles per hour but only in short bursts.

—*National Geographic* magazine

Competency	Example Behavior
Opportunity development	o Creates opportunities through conversations with clients and partners o Creates innovative solutions to solve clients' problems o Communicates effectively orally or in writing o Identifies new or expanded business opportunities o Meets regularly with clients, prospective clients, and partners o Qualifies opportunities through research, conversation, and follow-up o Exhibits persistence and is not easily stopped o Is disciplined in follow-up o Understands our value proposition and offerings o Understands the marketplace and procurement practices of clients o Conveys credibility with clients

Capture management	o Ensures organization is optimally positioned to win a specific new business opportunity
	o Creates distinctions and articulates differentiations with competition
	o Creates innovative, compelling solutions that leverage our offerings and organizational strengths
	o Able to synthesize multiple ideas, disciplines, and stakeholders
	o Creates compelling teaming strategies that offer a differentiated solution for the opportunity
	o Develops and executes capture strategy
	o Drives pricing strategy and ensures technical and pricing strategy are consistent and mutually supportive
	o Negotiates successful arrangements with partners that create a winning team
	o Communicates effectively both internally and externally
	o Makes good decisions about pursuing, bidding, and winning new opportunity
	o Supports communication and team cohesiveness in proposal team
Proposal development	o Integrates understanding, technical approach, management approaches, personnel, and corporate experience into a cohesive, compelling story
	o Prepares effective storyboards and translates into effective proposal text
	o Able to articulate feature/benefits pairs of our proposal approaches
	o Thrives in high-intensity, deadline-driven environment
	o Skilled in defining and communicating proposal win themes and discriminators
	o Skilled in conveying concepts in both graphics and prose

06

PEOPLE LEADERSHIP

The good-to-great leaders [level 5 leaders] seem to have come from Mars. Self-effacing, quiet, reserved, even shy—these leaders are a paradoxical blend of humility and professional will.

—Jim Collins, *Good to Great*

Simply put, effective leaders cause people to follow. This is the one common thread I can find in my life experience and study of leadership. Beyond that, there are innumerable styles, categories, and approaches to leading people. There is not a single formula or one style, though increasingly styles of leadership that worked fifty or even twenty years ago in a certain context are proving increasingly ineffective or unsustainable today.

It's not my intention to provide a treatise on people leadership. As I mentioned at the beginning of this book, there are countless books, seminars, and courses on effectively leading people. But what I do hope to do in this chapter is share what I have learned about effective people leadership as it fits in the broader context of the Complete Business Leader framework.

A leader is not on the journey to becoming a Complete Business Leader unless he or she has mastered (or more appropriately, is mastering) the dimension of *People Leadership*. In an organizational sense, Complete Business Leaders optimize the value of the organization's human capital by causing those human beings to follow and to succeed in their jobs.

Over the years, I have seen and experienced highly effective people leaders, as well as ineffective ones. In the Complete Business Leader framework, I have captured and will describe below what I think are the key competencies and the specific behaviors demonstrating those competencies that are practiced by effective people leaders.

And just to clarify, I would say I have yet to find a single leader who has attained complete mastery of all of these competencies—certainly not me. Throughout this chapter I refer to examples of people leaders. As with other chapters, I will generally use their name if it was a positive example, and if a negative example, I will generally not use the name unless it is a well-known public figure.

As I noted just above here, the standard of what constitutes an effective style of people leadership is evolving. Take the example of General George Patton from WWII. By most measures, he was actually an effective people leader for his time. He caused large groups of people to work together, rely on each other, and march straight into the face of likely death. By his own admission, General Patton was a mean, ornery fellow who led by fear. He was also certainly neither self-effacing nor humble, so he definitely didn't fit the level 5 leadership definition by Jim Collins. Patton was self-absorbed and narcissistic and an awful human being. I postulate that his set of leadership behaviors would not be nearly as effective in today's military, and it certainly doesn't work in the modern business context.

Before we dive into specific competencies, I'll give one general example of a person who met many of the competencies I'll highlight below.

I have referred to Don Holzworth quite a few times now in the book. Don was not a perfect leader, and by his own self-awareness and admission, not a perfect people leader. Yet, as I have pondered at length about these *People Leadership* competencies and measured Don against them, the clear reality is that he was an effective people leader:

- o Don had a keen eye for talent and managed to get that talent to work and produce for him. He also managed to get that talent to gel as an effective team. Don didn't overpay or over incentivize, but he compensated enough to keep his key leaders intact through a nine-year growth spurt at a 150 percent combined annual growth rate.
- o Don developed people, including me. He was sometimes harsh and always candid with his feedback, but over time most of his team came to realize that he genuinely cared about us achieving our own potential. He didn't praise often, so when he did, you knew you had done something really great.
- o Don delegated effectively. He came to know what he was good and not good at. And in that regard, he was very self-aware. He gathered people around him who could do things he couldn't or wouldn't. And he got the right people in the right seats at the leadership level.
- o Don led by example. He demonstrated characteristics of moving to action, producing results, and effectively allocating time and resources. And Don did what he

said he was going to do. If he spoke it, he generally delivered it.

o And toward the end of our nine-year run, Don mostly stepped back and let a couple of us run the company day to day.

Below I'll describe four major competencies of *People Leadership* (selection, development, delegation, and example) and example behaviors and characteristics of each. In trying to shed light on these competencies, I'll again use examples of leaders I have observed and learned from and vignettes of positive and negative examples of people leadership. In several places, I'll use Don as an example.

COMPETENCIES OF PEOPLE LEADERSHIP

SELECTION. Complete Business Leaders recruit and hire talented people who fit the organization's needs and values. Some leaders do this by a highly rigorous analytical process, while others select on gut. Regardless of their methods, effective people leaders are magnets for "A" talent, knowing that A talent attracts more A talent.

Many state-of-the-practice HR professionals will call for systematic behavioral-based hiring, rigorous testing, and numerous rounds of group interviews. I don't have an issue with these approaches, but in my experience, I haven't seen it produce reliably higher-caliber talent. Leaders—not processes and systems—spot talent.

I have been trained and worked in and around these state-of-the-practice HR approaches. In my view, while these systems and processes are helpful, it still comes down to a judgment call on whether a particular person is the right talent for the context.

In fact, in hiring a new leader to work for me, I use the Complete Business Leader framework's competencies as a lens to evaluate new leadership talent. But I don't systematically score things, tally up totals, and hire based on a score. Similar to other CBL dimensions, my philosophy is find and adopt good, rigorous processes AND not just blindly follow them.

Back to my old wizard, Gandalf: He was an exquisite selector of talent. In The Lord of the Rings, Gandalf selected talent in the right size and mix. None of the other characters seemed to understand why Gandalf put so much trust in hobbits and wanted them on his "leadership team." Yet over the course of the expansive Lord of the Rings trilogy, it became clear why each person had been selected. It was exactly the right leaders for exactly that time.

And Gandalf got them to work as a team. In addition to recruiting and hiring talent, Complete Business Leaders build effective teams. It comes to naught to gather loads of A talent if they are ill-suited to the organizational context or can't be inspired to work together effectively. Under any leader other than Gandalf, the Fellowship of the Ring probably would have splintered, faltered, or all died long before the mission to destroy the ring was completed.

Again, there are those far more learned than I who have researched and written amazingly on how to build effective teams. I highly recommend resources such as *The Five Dysfunctions of a Team* by Patrick Lencioni or *Building Effective Teams* by Duke Corporate Education. What my own experience has taught me is that it starts with spotting and hiring A talent that fits the organization's needs and values and culminates with a leader doing whatever it takes to cause that set of A talent to succeed as a team.

As I look back on my own career, one of my greatest successes and fulfillments as a leader was building the executive team I had at Futures Group. That team was surely diverse: three white men (including me as the leader), one black man, and three women. Each had their own amazing talents, and they sometimes bristled with each other. Several of them were highly credentialed (two medical doctors and two PhDs) and well connected in the market; they were all scary smart, and some could be prickly. Any one of them could have walked out and been highly marketable immediately. And honestly, they didn't all like each other.

Yet we managed to hold together as a team and lead Futures Group through several years of very turbulent market seas, reestablish the firm's rightful place as one of the world's leaders in health policy, rebuild its brand, and grow the business into new areas. Together they were an amazing team, able to achieve way more than they thought possible.

In building this team piece by piece over several years, it took every bit of learning, experience, creativity, finesse, and inspiration I could muster to hold them together as a team. In the end, we sold the company because it was the right time to do so. And I was heartbroken to depart from them.

One of those Futures Group leaders, Shannon Hader, was one of the best I have worked with at spotting talent and forming effective teams. When I hired Shannon to run a part of the company, the team she inherited was dysfunctional. They had uneven talent and little direction and focus; they were frequently working at cross-purposes with each other and groups in other parts of the company. Within a year,

Shannon restructured the team, replaced several members, promoted others, and had the team beginning to operate with common purpose. I also came to trust Shannon's judgment on talent for other roles outside her accountability area.

DEVELOPMENT. The second major competency of great people leaders is how they develop people. Great people leaders cause the people following them to grow and develop far beyond what would have ever happened just in the normal course of events. The end result is sometimes—many times—that the mentee surpasses the mentor. That's when a true people leader knows he or she has succeeded.

To develop people, you absolutely must provide frank, frequent, honest feedback. This feedback should be both positive (reinforcing) and negative (corrective). This is notoriously hard for both the leader and the person being led. It is a rare human being that likes to give or receive negative feedback. But there is simply no alternative. Giving feedback is a behavior that can be learned through practice. It's like a muscle: the more you exercise it, the less painful it is when you use it. Frank, frequent, honest feedback presumes a level of trust and vulnerability. This doesn't just happen naturally. The leader has to set the context and take the first step to create trust and vulnerability (see Chapter 2, *Individual Wisdom*).

I mentioned previously in the book that early in my career, I almost got fired. I had become an expert in corporate finance and business but had moved back into a technical line management role and struggled to adjust and perform well as a technical manager. I remember when a retired general, who was my boss's boss's boss, called me into his office and said, "Chris, maybe nobody else has told you this, but you are not cutting it." He went on to give me specific examples. It was the harshest feedback I have ever received. I thought many of the examples were unfair and misinformed, but the conversation did move me to action. I took a bunch of actions quickly to leverage my corporate relationships, refocus my efforts, and prove him wrong. Somehow, he managed to find and hit a deep nerve (insecurity) within me that I was not big or strong enough. I resolved to prove him wrong.

My general response to people who doubted me has always been, "Fine, I will show you. I'll outwork you." As I thought about that feedback session more in the succeeding days and weeks, I realized that while his specifics may have been off, his general feedback was worth at least considering. By the way, he was a not a particularly nice person, but notice that I never forgot that feedback, which propelled me to be better.

A related and necessary behavior of great people leaders is ensuring the employees feel heard and respected in those difficult conversations. This can take the form of bilateral feedback, or it can be a leader having to give hard or bad news (e.g., you are not performing and we have to let you go, or we are promoting someone over you). I know what it is like having to give that hard news. Ultimately, a great people leader must do hard things and have hard conversations (see Chapter 3, *Relationship Management*).

A recent example of this is back to my beloved Clemson Tigers football team. Head Coach Dabo Swinney has had to make lots of hard decisions and have lots of hard conversations over his time as head coach, as I noted in an earlier chapter. I would guess that none were harder than a recent situation when he had to inform his starting quarterback, Kelly Bryant, that he would no longer be starting. Kelly had been with the program for more than four years, was a really good player and team leader, was popular with fans, and had waited his turn to start. But then an upstart eighteen-year-old, who was just freakishly talented, won the job.

Dabo has said that he loves Kelly Bryant like a son. I think the coach had the difficult conversation with Kelly because it was in the best interest of the team and maybe also in the long term in the best interest of Kelly himself. Kelly probably doesn't think this is true today, but maybe someday he might.

Making the choice to have the difficult conversation is not enough though. The great people leader must deliver that conversation while ensuring the recipient of the information feels heard and respected. This means it is not a one-way monologue. It means the leader has to then listen with empathy and authentic caring for the recipient. Most people recognize that businesses (or football teams) are not democracies and that someone ultimately has to make the final difficult decisions. But the organization and its people are more resilient when people feel heard and respected.

Of course, I wasn't in the locker room when Coach Swinney told Kelly Bryant that he had lost his starting job, but I believe that Dabo then heard Kelly out with empathy and love, like a father would. Even though Bryant still chose to leave the team after that talk, he left having been giving the opportunity to have his voice heard.

Another key element of developing people is mentoring them actively to achieve and grow professionally. Of course, frank, frequent, honest feedback is a pathway to helping the person grow professionally, as is leading by example (more on this later in this chapter). Sometimes, effective development of an employee results in the employee leaving the tutelage of the mentor to make it on their own. As I noted earlier, for a true people leader, there is almost no greater professional fulfillment than to see one of their stars end up having even greater success than the mentor did.

I have a couple of examples of this. Coach Nick Saban, head coach of Alabama's college football team, is unquestionably the most successful football coach living today. He has created a juggernaut that is almost unbeatable (except twice by my Clemson Tigers in national championship games in the past three years!), and, as of this writing, has won six national championships.

Possibly more important and more impactful in the long term, Saban has now spawned ten other college football head coaches, eight of whom are active head coaches today. These are former assistant coaches who came along under his tutelage and eventually were hired away to be head coaches. In fact, Saban has recently had to face a few of his old assistant coaches. On the field, those mentees of Nick Saban are stars now in their own right.

A second example is one back in my work environment. Some years ago when I was with Constella, we acquired a small company that then was absorbed into the unit I was leading. There was a young leader, Paul Nedzbala, in the acquired company who had some raw strengths but was a bit rough around the edges. At first I was not sure how it would work with Paul reporting to me, but over time we developed a strong rapport based on trust and respect.

Over several years, we worked closely together, with me giving him frank, frequent, authentic feedback. I saw tremendous potential in him and began to see him as one of my possible successors, so I groomed him hard. One of the great things about Paul was that he was so welcoming of feedback and anxious to grow professionally. He was like a sponge (this relates to continuous learning from Chapter 2, the *Individual Wisdom* dimension!). He listened to feedback and evolved into an increasingly more Complete Business Leader. This dynamic with Paul was not without challenges, though, as some his peers began to question whether I was showing favoritism to Paul. This caused me to have to have other frank conversations as well.

As noted earlier, we eventually sold Constella to a large publicly traded company. I stayed for a year and then led a management buyout of Futures Group. Paul stayed with the company that had acquired Constella Group. Over the eleven years since then, Paul has survived and thrived in at least two successive mergers, each time expanding his role, and is now running a $3 billion business unit! He has far surpassed me in terms of size and scale of his leadership. I am so happy for him and honored to have played some part in his success.

Finally, in developing people, a Complete Business Leader inspires people to achieve more than they thought possible. This inspiration can manifest in multiple ways. It doesn't always have to be with rah-rah locker room–style speeches, though there is nothing wrong with that. This inspiration is hard to exactly define and codify; rather, it has to be felt.

In general, I think it boils down to a leader's intangible *way of being* (see again Chapter 2, *Individual Wisdom*) that causes people to believe in their own greatness, not the greatness of the leader. That intangible way of being causes people to see beyond typical roadblocks and barriers to imagine what is possible and be inspired to do uncommon things in order to achieve the possible. That intangible way of being causes people to believe in themselves and each other. And the ultimate success of the Complete Business

Leader is when people no longer need the leader around to be inspired—when they can generate that inspiration and belief on their own.

As a leader, Ronald Reagan exemplified this inspiration. Of course, he was not universally loved and had some views and policies that seemed harsh for some. However, he inspired me and tens of millions of others to believe in a bright possible future. I came of age to adulthood under Reagan. His *way of being* connected with people at their core. We began to believe it was "morning in America" again. We began to believe in that "shining city on a hill" known as America. More important than the vague, pleasant patriotism underpinning that, Reagan inspired us to achieve. We saw the possibility to have economic prosperity, global security, and peace all together. We began to believe in ourselves and what we could achieve together.

Global economic growth and prosperity? No problem. Outspending, out innovating, and outworking the Soviets until their communist society crumbled? Absolutely. Even when faced with adversity, such as the Challenger explosion in 1986, Reagan inspired us to believe we could rebound and achieve even greater things. For many, the Reagan era was a time of positive energy, calls for greatness, and belief that our future was bright. Reagan embodied the viewpoint of American exceptionalism.

DELEGATION. A third major competency for *People Leadership* is delegation. To delegate means to parse out work, activities, or roles to others (obvious definition). Complete Business Leaders don't just delegate; they delegate *effectively*. To delegate *effectively* means to parse out *appropriate* work to *appropriate* people and cause them to be successful in achieving the results you wanted and couldn't have achieved without them. So let's unpack that a bit.

To delegate effectively, you must empower people with the authority and resources needed to achieve a result. You must then hold them accountable or better yet let them hold themselves responsible (see Chapter 2, *Individual Wisdom* again) for achieving the result expected. Sounds straightforward right?

One of the most common mistakes I have seen leaders and organizations make is having a mismatch between the level of empowerment and the level of accountability. In other words, a mismatch happens when a leader is empowered to make a set of decisions via a particular role but is not held accountable for the results of decisions made, or vice versa, when a leader is held accountable for a role or result but was not empowered to really do what was needed to achieve that result. Another way to look at this is when input costs (money, human resources, or both) are managed by someone different than the person responsible for the consequences or outputs of those input costs.

At times, I have violated my own principle around matching empowerment with accountability. This has happened most frequently when I have empowered a leader or leaders to make decisions that require spending money without first setting up the structures where they have a profit and loss (P&L) accountability or an expense budget or other related metrics. Without that counterbalance of accountability for the cost of, say, hiring three consultants or spending loads on travel or other ways to spend money, it's free money. When there is no constraint on spending whatever it takes to achieve a result, there is no need to balance the costs with the results.

That leads me to a related characteristic of effective delegation: articulating clear responsibilities and expectations. When someone is clear on their scope and what they are responsible for, they generally feel more empowered to act. And when someone is clear on the result or outcome that is expected of them, they generally feel more ownership for that result and behave differently.

The military is extremely adept at being clear on responsibilities and expected outcomes. In fact, the military pioneered division of duties, delegation, and accountability in the world of organizational development.

Other organizations such as Jack Welch's GE became world renowned and imitated by many in how GE structured clear management roles and how they set and managed expectations. The GE of today may have lost its way from a strategy standpoint, but operational execution through rigorous operational management is still a hallmark. People were always clear on what was expected of them and how they would be measured against those expectations.

As with many management principles, clear delegation and accountability around results is well understood, documented, and taught in any business management course. Actually carrying this out effectively is not only a *management* discipline but more important is a *leadership* endeavor.

I have found that in global health development and research markets where I have worked, which tend to be less hard-nosed and business driven, it takes a distinct kind of leadership to put these structures of delegation and accountability for results in place and cause employees to buy into them. That's why I address this as a people leadership issue.

In my line of work, I interact regularly with nonprofit organizations, including some very large ones. I also deal frequently with academic institutions. Nonprofit employees tend to align to the mission of their organization. Academia tend to align around professor-driven research agendas. These alignments are noble and bring out passion and commitment, yet neither of these comports well naturally to effective delegation, clear expectation setting, and accountability for results. Some nonprofits and academic institutions struggle with lack of role clarity, ineffective delegation, and inconsistency in holding people accountable for results. This rigor is deemed too businesslike, too harsh, or a distraction to the nonprofit mission or academic research agenda.

Another example of this is in faith-based organizations, including churches and faith-based nonprofits. As my daughter, the seminary student, says, leaders in faith-based organizations tend to be "F's" (Feelers) on the Myers–Briggs scale, rather than "T's" (Thinkers). Feelers have a hard time holding others to cold, hard accountabilities.

Nonprofits, academia, and faith-based organizations, of course, want to produce results that are aligned to their missions. And just to be clear, many aspects of Complete Business Leadership are not about producing profit; they are really about helping organizations create value by achieving the results for which they exist to achieve, whether that is saving lives, saving souls, creating jobs, or making peoples' lives easier.

When defining clear responsibilities and expected outcomes, the Complete Business Leader sets high yet realistic standards and expectations. Getting the balance between high and realistic is part operational management rigor and strategic management alignment and part leadership art. A great people leader inspires his or her teams to strive for and achieve things they didn't previously think possible. And that great people leader knows when the bar is set so high that employees can no longer see the possible and would be demoralized by a completely unachievable goal.

For example, going into a new year and setting an annual business development growth target for your sales teams that has no grounding in the reality of the current market dynamics, the current positioning of the organization, or any pre-sales lead development will actually demotivate rather than inspire people to achieve.

On the other hand, the transformational CDC contract that my old boss Don Holzworth convinced his team to pursue (see Chapter 2, *Individual Wisdom*) was initially deemed as completely unwinnable by his teams, but actually Don knew the market dynamics and what his team was capable of. He just needed to convince the team of that!

Another example is when Craig Venter and his private enterprise, Celera Genomics, set out in a race with the US government to sequence the human genome. The government launched a fifteen-year program called the Human Genome Project. Many didn't believe it was possible ever or at least in our lifetime. Others, including government scientific leaders, estimated it would take more than the fifteen years to accomplish. Venter and his team blew that away by achieving it three years ahead of schedule. Venter may have set a high bar, but he had enough grounding in the science and confidence in the talents of his scientists and faith in the progression of computing technology to believe it was possible himself. Then he inspired his teams to believe it was possible.

Delegating effectively is one of the ultimate indicators of a great people leader. When done well, aligning responsibilities to other individuals who are capable of or have the potential to achieve a set of expectations that come with those responsibilities is a gift of generosity (see also Chapter 2, *Individual Wisdom*). It offers the opportunity for the delegate to fulfill their potential for greatness. It not only gets stuff done that wouldn't otherwise get done, it opens whole new possibilities for the delegate to see themselves in a new light, to strive and work toward something, to deliver new value to the world.

EXAMPLE. The final competency of great people leaders is leading by example. Alexander the Great led by example, as did Julius Caesar. Alexander went out for three years with his men, slept in tents with them, ate and drank with them, and fought alongside them. Caesar did, as well, at least in the earlier part of his life. It was Caesar at the front of his legions on his horse when he crossed the Rubicon River.

Jim Boomgard, the CEO of DAI where I currently am building out a new business, leads by example. Jim lived and worked for ten years in a DAI field office and ran projects from a *long* way (in Indonesia) outside of US headquarters. He has also worked alongside people to write winning proposals. He has made all the easy and hard decisions required of a leader over the years. So he has "street cred" with employees. There is virtually nothing he would ask someone to take on that he hasn't already done himself.

A great people leader is action and results oriented. People respond to decisiveness and forward action. Employees don't respond well to inaction. Different people leaders have different styles, of course; however, in my experience, while employees like to be consulted and involved in decision making, more important, they value forward movement. If leaders want others to be results oriented, they have to lead by example by being results oriented as well. That means leaders holding themselves fully responsible for results produced or not produced.

Part of leading by example is also living company values and codes of conduct and following company systems and processes. There is almost nothing more demotivating to employees than a leader championing all of these things—values, conduct, company policies and processes—and then not following them himself or herself.

Sadly, I have witnessed this in some of our US political leaders, as well as other leaders I have encountered in business and other governments, such as when a US government leader calls on all staff to save on travel costs and follow arcane federal travel regulations but then charters a private plane for his own travel, or when a developing country leader waxes about stomping out corruption throughout his government yet lines his foreign bank account with millions in kickbacks for oil deals. When leaders think they are outside the norms and laws of their own organizations, it undermines the very unifying fabric binding the organization.

Effective leaders also set a strong example by being effective with their time. As a reminder from an earlier chapter: money is easy to replace and people are hard to replace, whereas time is the one irreplaceable resource in life—at least until someone invents time travel. Employees respect leaders who manage their time well and who value others' time. Employees want a leader who respects that an employee's time has value. Of course, a leader's effective hourly rate might be way higher and the leader has to balance lots of priorities, but time is just as irreplaceable for the employee as it is for the leader.

Two of my personality quirks are that I am impatient (as my family reminds me frequently) and I am habitually on time. Anyone who works with me knows that I am absolutely hardcore about being on time, including starting and ending meetings on time. Sometimes this works as a positive leadership characteristic and sometimes it gets in the way of my being effective.

One of the things that drives me crazy about my frequent visits to see government officials is waiting for long periods of time a ministry official's outer office. It's a common scene: a couple of my colleagues and I are escorted into an outer waiting area with couches, a TV on low volume playing local news, and a desk with an assistant. We get there fifteen minutes early for our meeting. And we wait. And wait. And forty-five minutes later, another handler from the inner office comes out and says to the assistant in the waiting area, "ABC will see you now." And we are escorted in then for the now fifteen minutes we have left with the Minister of ABC or some other dignitary.

What I am left with in this common scenario is that the minister thinks his or her time is more valuable than ours. This could be because the official has been coddled as a government official with handlers and assistants. It could just be a simple power play—I will make you wait to see me because I am more important and valuable than you. My take on it, though, is it's disrespectful of the other human being and wastes everybody's irreplaceable minutes of life. So don't do that as a leader!

Once, years ago when I was meeting with my coach, Jane Smith, we got on the subject of time management and priorities. I was saying how important something was, and she asked me what amount time I devoted to it and at what time of day. Then she said people can say things are a priority but the way you know what someone's real priorities are is to observe where they spend their time.

So don't say that family is a top priority if you don't carve out quantity (as well as quality) time. And what things get your focus when you are at your best, not at the end of the day when you are exhausted? Quality time is when you are at your best and can give total focus to something. For me that is 6:00–9:00 a.m. For others, like my millennial daughter, this seems to be 10:00 p.m.–1:00 a.m. Maybe by the time she is fifty-four like me, her best time will be 6:00 a.m.? So if a leader is setting an example, then the way she spends her time and energy is aligned with her stated priorities.

A wizard is never late. Nor is he early; he arrives precisely when he means to.
—Gandalf, *The Fellowship of the Ring* movie

Gandalf the Wizard led by example. He was reflective and seeking of input, yet when it came time to move, he was decisive and results oriented. He saw, always, many possible pathways to achieve something and work through others to achieve it, but he knew at his core there was a time to move. Others followed his lead.

He also "walked the talk." He didn't just talk about core values and codes of conduct—he lived them himself so others could see and follow. He refused to succumb to the temptations of additional powers offered him by evil wizards (Saruman and Sauron) and refused to take shortcuts that would have been easier for him. Finally, Gandalf was really clear about time management and aligning how he spent his time with what his priorities were. Sometimes it might have seemed like Gandalf was spending time on needless things, but he had a reason for exactly how he spent every moment.

SUMMARY COMMENTS

So in this dimension of the Complete Business Leader, *People Leadership*, we have discussed four key competencies—selection, development, delegation, and example—and their characteristics and behaviors.

These competencies are interrelated and mutually necessary to be a Complete Business Leader. The Complete Business Leader who has mastery of *People Leadership* will be exceptional at selecting talent, developing that talent, delegating and setting expectations for that talent, and setting a leadership example for that talent.

There is an immense body of work documented on managing people. Much (though not all) of this work has validity and can be useful. Fundamentally, though, leading people—causing people to follow—is a leadership endeavor that requires you to bring your best self.

Some followers may expect their leaders to be perfect and without flaw, but my experience is most followers in organizations recognize that their leaders also human. Followers do expect their leaders to bring the best in themselves as leaders and bring out the best in followers.

It's a challenge to bring it every day in every situation. As flawed human beings, leaders bring baggage with them in how they lead. Great people leaders manage to hone the competencies described above and cause people to follow, even in the face of their own baggage. Sometimes as a leader, your baggage has to be recognized and named to be able to set it aside for the moment and bring your best self. That doesn't mean we rid ourselves of the baggage, though sometimes that would be nice; it means we know it is there and can choose what to do with it. And this awareness requires *Individual Wisdom* (see Chapter 2).

Competency	Example Behavior
Selection	o Recruits and hires talented people who fit the organization's needs and values o Builds effective teams
Development	o Provides praise and critique of employee performance o Inspires employees to achieve more than they thought they could o Develops and mentors people to grow professionally o Provides frequent, honest coaching and feedback o Has difficult conversations with employees while ensuring they feel heard and respected
Delegation	o Articulates clear responsibilities, expected outcomes, and accountabilities o Delegates effectively, empowering people while holding them accountable o Sets high but realistic standards and expectations of staff
Example	o Is action and results oriented o Follows company employee performance management systems and processes o Is an effective time manager o Demonstrates company values, code of conduct, and effective management

07

PROJECT MANAGEMENT

I have always found that plans are useless, but planning is indispensable.

—Gen. Dwight D. Eisenhower

Operation Overlord (code name for the Allied invasion of Normandy on D-Day) is the largest amphibious assault ever attempted. Considered by most historians as the turning point in World War II, the operation required more than two years of intricate planning. In fact, though the overall goal didn't change during that period, the specific plans changed numerous times. When the "project" finally came to fruition, more than 195,000 troops, 7,000 ships and landing craft, and 11,000 aircraft were involved on D-Day, according to the US National Archives.[15]

The logistical feat of planning and coordinating not only those directly involved but the hundreds of thousands of support personnel and other resources is unprecedented. The staging area in Great Britain alone required intricately coordinated fuel, food, ammunition, clothing, and security supply chains and logistics. The planning also included intelligence gathering, practice landings and other training, and a massive deception of the German enemy regarding when and where the invasion would occur. All of this planning had to be accomplished in secret.[16] Operation Overlord is still studied today for learnings as a major planning and logistics accomplishment, a massive "project management" effort.

Other famous efforts studied by project management specialists include the Boston "Big Dig" project (officially titled the Central Artery/Tunnel Project), which involved a nearly twenty-year effort to build an underground expressway and tunnel system without bringing bustling downtown Boston to a halt. The project covered 7.8 miles, creating 161 lane miles of highway, about half of which was in tunnels under water. The final cost was $14.8 billion against an original target at project conception of $2.6 to $4.4 billion.[17] The Boston Big Dig is considered on the scale of other massive infrastructure projects, including the building of the Panama Canal and the "Chunnel" connecting Great Britain to the European continent via tunnel under the English Channel.

The Boston Big Dig ended up taking considerably longer and costing significantly more than originally conceived. However, by almost all results metrics, the project modernized the city, dramatically reduced wasteful commute time, kept the city a thriving downtown for commerce and tourism, reconnected nearby neighborhoods to the city, and created numerous new parks and other green spaces.

The Complete Business Leader must have mastery of managing projects on time, within budget, and with high quality. *Project Management* is an essential dimension in most any business or organizational endeavor. The Complete Business Leader may not manage projects day to day but must fundamentally understand and make decisions about projects or large corporate initiatives based on a set of *Project Management* competencies.

Optimizing the triangle of schedule, cost, and quality has confounded all managers of projects, including Operation Overlord and the Big Dig. Yet this is what managers are tasked to do. Skeptics say you can have any two of the three legs of the project management triangle but not all three. The mathematician in me, however, knows that there is a formula that optimizes all three, as long as there are constraints on all three variables. If any one of the variables is unconstrained, then control of the other two variables breaks down.

Much of my own learning about project management came from on-the-job training—learning by doing. I learned first under the tutelage my first boss, Frank O'Brien, a retired Army lieutenant colonel. I learned and applied many aspects of project management later from another boss, Frank Wilkinson. I am grateful for learning from both of them.

Then at Constella Group during my time as chief operating officer, I put together and launched a documented project management methodology. Highlights of what you'll see in the rest of this chapter come from my own experience, which were then documented in Constella Group's Project Management Methodology. In the Complete Business Leader context, I'll describe project management as a leadership endeavor.

By the way, I'll warn you in advance it is possible you'll find this chapter a bit tedious, as it addresses some more hands-on skills that most would say are technical project management skills, though I describe them through a lens of leadership competencies. I encourage you to plow through it and see if you don't come away seeing project management as a leadership endeavor.

COMPETENCIES OF PROJECT MANAGEMENT

As with other dimensions of the CBL, I have structured a set of competencies characterized by specific behaviors that can be learned and practiced in the area of *Project Management*. Also, as with other parts of the CBL, I will not try to duplicate here what is taught in numerous other books and courses around the discipline of project management.

If you've taken any formal training on project management or even sat for the PMP (Project Management Professional) certification created by the Project Management Institute, you'll recognize some of the key skill sets here, though my specific take on them is from my own experience as a project manager and then as a leader of project managers. As with all aspects of the CBL, I'll describe *Project Management* competencies from a leadership lens: organized, disciplined, analytical, and communication.

ORGANIZED. An essential competency of effective project management is being organized (see also Chapter 2, *Individual Wisdom*). Some people have clean desks, structured folders, neat to-do lists, risk trackers, and detailed calendars. Other people do a lot of this in their heads or via unorthodox means. Regardless of the tactical approaches, the organized project manager has to be able to intake, process, and integrate lots of detail. This detail needs to be organized and maintained in a way that ensures ongoing decision-making, course correction, and allocation of resources.

In addition to managing detail, the Complete Business Leader and effective project manager has to use that detail to understand and make decisions on the interdependencies among schedule, cost, and quality on a project, optimizing these three coequal aspects.

For example, over-resourcing a particular activity may run up project cost. Sometimes over-resourcing can ensure an activity gets done quicker (but not always) and sometimes it can ensure an activity gets done with higher quality (but not always). Sometimes, however, over-resourcing an activity is the right thing to do if that activity is the linchpin thing on which the rest of the project depends and if cost can be made up elsewhere.

In Operation Overlord, Eisenhower had to balance how much human resources to plan for in the initial D-Day invasion. He had to balance schedule, cost, and quality. Over-resource it with troops from other war theaters and you might lose ground on other fronts, resulting in costs or delay elsewhere and possibly undermining the overall goal of defeating the Axis powers. Over-resourcing could also result in more chaos than necessary on the battlefield. Under-resource it and the effort may fail. Eisenhower and his leadership team also had to plan—not just the number of human resources but the *right* numbers of the *right* kinds of skills and at the *right* time.

Incidentally, Eisenhower's job for D-Day was further complicated by having to coordinate across his other war partners, primarily the British.[18]

In my work world of global health projects, the fate of the free world is not at stake, of course, but the stakes are pretty high sometimes. With the companies I have been involved in, our project teams know that our work can make a positive difference in the health of individuals, communities, and populations. And we do this with external institutional partners in almost all projects. Sometimes it is maddening and seemingly a waste of time to coordinate with partners. But the weight of evidence shows that in complex areas like global health, no one organization has all the right resources or solutions. It is better to partner. So I advise our teams to learn how to coordinate projects with external partners. If Eisenhower could effectively coordinate with his British colleagues, so can we. See also Chapter 3, *Relationship Management.*

A critical component of effective project management is the detail job of breaking down a project into successively granular levels of activities. One of the biggest challenges of effectively delivering a project is accurately estimating the clock time and level of effort needed to complete chunks of activities and the dependencies among those chunks of work leading to project completion.

Breaking down the work to be accomplished into what the project management professional community calls a "work breakdown structure," or WBS, is part rigor, part art, and part experience. In whatever way a project manager does it, the project must be broken down into the lowest level activities possible where the duration and level of effort can be accurately estimated and then tracked. There are plenty of tools to help in this effort (see next competency). The key is to not shortchange this painstaking effort. This is what it means to be organized.

Over the years, I have heard many reasons for people not doing the tedious work of breaking down and estimating the work activities, such as, "This project is too nebulous to break into WBS elements," or "Chris, you don't understand the nature of *our* kinds of projects. Our projects are too big, too complex, too . . ." (you can fill in the blanks). I challenge this notion.

The Boston Big Dig used work breakdown structures. I can only imagine how many lines of WBS elements there were! Of course, that project was way over budget and took way longer than originally planned, but I postulate that it would have cost five times more and maybe still not be complete had the project managers not applied the discipline of breaking down the work into measurable activities and then estimating and tracking them.

A related key component of being organized is optimizing the allocation of human resources to project activities. This is, again, part organized rigor and part leadership art. Human resources are inputs into the production of a project. But human resources are, after all, humans. That means they are fallible, have bad days, bring their personal issues to work, and get overcommitted. Sometimes they quit and go to another job. So the organized project manager has to take these kinds of things into account when planning and managing work activities associated with a project.

You can't just allocate sixteen hours of a mid-level statistician, twenty-four hours of a junior researcher, and eight hours of a data scientist. You might know that in a perfect world, even based on past experience, it will take this many hours of these kinds of people to complete a critical activity. But then the data scientist gets sick for three days, the junior researcher breaks up with his partner and is useless at work for a time, and the statistician decides another piece of work is more professionally intriguing and doesn't get your activity done.

For the record, I have had each of these examples happen to me on projects in real life. The most maddening one was the statistician who just decided that a piece of work for a pharmaceutical clinical trial was not intellectually stimulating enough and didn't want to do the work! The organized business leader should expect and pre-seed alternative approaches to accomplish the work when the project activity plan does not go exactly as originally laid out.

Back to my favorite wizard: Gandalf continuously recalculated the next set of steps based on adverse or unplanned events, such as trolls showing up unexpectedly!

A final key characteristic of being organized in the project management realm is keeping good, rigorous files and documentation. Again, some good project managers I have worked with didn't naturally like to take the time to keep good files, but in my experience, this is critical for the success of projects.

Projects are a team sport. They almost always require coordinating with others, showing documentation to clients, ensuring projects can keep going if team members move on. All of these are aided by having good filing. In the project management methodology I documented and launched for Constella Group, I called this the "project management notebook." It was actually structured electronic file folders sharable with among project teams. There are numerous good automated tools now for aiding in project management documentation.

In the pharmaceutical clinical trials industry I worked in for a few years, this set of project files was not only good discipline for the above reasons, it was mandatory from a regulatory standpoint. Our project files were subject to inspection and audit at any time by the client or even by FDA as the regulator. If the files were poor, the pharma company client could terminate our contract or at a minimum penalize our project invoices. FDA could penalize the pharma company or even terminate the whole clinical trial based on a lack of good project documentation.

DISCIPLINED. A second key competency for the effective project manager (and Complete Business Leader) is being disciplined. As I have said earlier, project management (all leadership activities, really) is part scientific rigor and part art. Project management calls for "disciplined art."

One characteristic of being disciplined is being able to produce, read, and interpret PERT and Gantt representations of project schedule and status. For those not familiar, these are fancy project scheduling terms, but essentially Gantt shows all project activities laid out sequentially by their activity duration over time. PERT graphically shows the dependencies of project activities to each other and the critical path, sometimes called shortest path. Critical path is the linkage from activity to activity where if one activity slips by one unit of time (usually a day), then the whole project duration slips by that exact amount.

In my experience, project managers sometimes shortchange the planning and tracking time required—in other words, the discipline—to lay out Gantt and PERT representations of a project. Yet when done rigorously, these tools help projects to be delivered more consistently on time and within resource constraints.

I have sometimes used these representations to effectively push back on clients. Multiple times I have had to say to a client something like, "We have delivered this document to you and our schedule calls for your review and comments within five days. This report is on the critical path of completing our project. Every day we do not get your comments back is a day slippage in completing the project." It is harder for a client to argue this point if you have Gantt and PERT representations to show them and can effectively use them.

Another aspect of this "disciplined" *Project Management* competency is having at least a working knowledge of available project management tools. At my first company, BDM, we actually designed and programmed our own custom project management software, crazy as that seems today. Later we migrated to the now ubiquitous Microsoft Project (MS Project).

I learned how to use MS Project in the early 1990s as a trial by fire. I was working on a large complex proposal for a new project—this seems to be a consistent theme of my work life—with a hard submission date. The bid was for a large multiyear project, and in our proposal we had to show a detailed project plan and schedule for how we would accomplish the scope of work, including showing all the activity dependencies, resource allocations, and durations. Someone loaded a newly released piece of Microsoft software on my big desktop PC and said, "You have three days to build the detailed project plan. Figure it out." I laid out the project plan; it had, if I remember correctly, more than 1,000 work elements (WBS elements) when I was all done.

MS Project is easy to use and intuitive for most people, notwithstanding that most organizations that use it probably use 25 percent of its features. I think the days are past when a senior leader can say they are too senior to know how to use a tool like MS Project or at least conceptually understand the tool and its outputs.

My father was an engineering project manager. He led teams that designed textile manufacturing plants in the US and around the world. Still living and active at age eighty-eight now, my dad retired before the age of PCs and tools like MS Project. But he certainly would understand the key components of what a project management tool can do and would understand the value of a tool that could automate all the stuff he used to do by hand!

Another capability the effective project manager needs to master is the concept of earned value management (EVM). There are now whole courses, textbooks tools, and certifications on EVM, so I will not try to replicate those. My non-textbook description is: EVM is essentially a method to integrate project activities, activity-level cost, and activity-level schedule all together in one combined view of the project. The method helps project managers avoid the trap of focusing only on budget or only on completion of activities or only on overall schedule.

My boss Frank Wilkinson introduced me to EVM back in the early 1990s. Once I began to grasp the EVM approach and the tools, a bunch of light bulbs went on in my head. It is so beautiful and elegant! Today there are sophisticated tools and systems for EVM and even certification programs for EVM. I learned and implemented EVM with just MS Project, Excel, and graphs. The key elements of my approach to EVM are:

- o Break down the project into its smallest elements (WBS), budget all resources required at the activity level, then spread those costs over the expected duration of that activity. The elements have to be small enough and short enough in duration to be able to accurately budget them. When you roll activity-level budgets together, you can plot a Budgeted Cost of Work Scheduled (BCWS) cost curve over the project's duration.

o Then in the actual execution of the project, you track Actual Cost of Work Performed (ACWP). ACWP just represents the actual total project burn by activity. This data comes from your actual project accounting each period and can be graphed in a cost curve.

o At the end of each reporting period (usually monthly but on a short project this might be weekly), assign a percent complete to each activity in the WBS. For simplicity, what I have used in the past is just 0, 25, 50, 75, or 100 percent. If you have the project broken down into enough specific short-duration activities, this approach should work fine. You then apply that percent complete to the original budgeted cost for each WBS element and roll up the resulting amount across all WBS elements. We call that Actual Cost of Work Scheduled (ACWS). The plotted ACWS cost curve represents how much your project *should* have burned to complete the *actual* amount of work performed.

When you then graph all three of these curves—BCWS, ACWP, and ACWS—onto one graphic, you can see a full and evident picture of project progress. This includes not only actual spend against original budget but also what you should have spent to complete the work completed so far. In a project that is going exactly as planned in terms of work completed and budget spent to schedule, all three curves are aligned. In a single picture, you can tell whether the project is behind schedule, over budget, or both.

For ease of the reader, I am not including example graphs in the book, but if you are interested, please see www.thecompletebusinessleader.com for a few examples.

If you want to learn more about EVM and how to apply it in your organization, there are plenty of resources out there. For most reasonably sized projects (not the Big Dig!), EVM can be done in Excel or MS Project or a combination of the two, though for larger, more complex projects or groups of projects, software such as Primavera (now owned by Oracle) offers more robust and scalable features. I also have plenty of annotated templates developed over the years. Contact me at www.thecompletebusinessleader.com.

Finally, an effective project manager needs have at least a working knowledge of project cost accounting— that is, how costs accumulate and get applied on an individual project. This includes understanding all of the direct controllable cost inputs: labor costs; nonlabor costs such as travel and consumables; subcontractor costs; and any corporate costs that get applied, such as fringe benefit costs on labor, corporate overheads, or other service center costs out of the direct control of the project manager.

Different organizations have varying approaches to project accounting, but it is likely that the organization will apply some sort of corporate overheads to projects; therefore, it is critical that the project manager understand the basis upon which these costs are applied and anticipates them as part of total project cost.

A critical element of project accounting is understanding external costs such as subcontractors and consultants. It is critical that the project manager understand how these costs are accounted for against the project, when they are incurred, accrued, and expensed. Even if the organization does not accrue these project costs in advance of paying them, the project manager should set up his or her own accrual tracking to make sure that actual project costs reported are as close as possible to the work completed and that surprise costs don't come in late.

For the effective project manager, it is not enough to slough off this "accounting stuff" to a project accountant, though a quality project accountant can be a lifesaver for the project manager. The effective project manager is accountable for project cost and usually has the difficult task of balancing project costs, schedule, quality, client expectations, *and* company expectations to deliver an expected project-level net profit.

ANALYTICAL. A third key competency of effective project management is being analytical. An analytical way of thinking may be part innate but can also be taught. Systematically assessing situations, breaking down problems, collecting and sorting through data, defining and then interrogating assumptions, seeing trends, biases, and patterns, then reassembling these dynamics into larger conclusions and solutions—all are characteristics of an analytical way of thinking. As with any muscle, through regular training, stressing through exercise of the muscle, the muscle can become stronger and more toned.

An analytical project manager can see and grasp complexity, correlate detail into patterns, and then step back and see the big picture. That big picture includes understanding the interdependencies of tasks, people, and processes, contextual factors that influence results. That understanding helps the project manager optimize all factors to deliver projects on time, on budget, with high quality. (See also Chapter 2, *Individual Wisdom*.)

For example, a football quarterback at the height of his game, like Tom Brady, exhibits this analytical muscle. By the way, I really don't like the Patriots and pull against them in any game they are playing because I am so tired of seeing them win, but I admire the lethal precision with which they play!

Anyway, Brady has complete mastery of the playbook at his disposal to run; he knows his players better than they know themselves and knows exactly what each player is going to do in every situation. The processes he goes through on any one play or series of plays is like breathing for him in terms of the progression of his reads of the defense and his understanding of the state of the game and time clock. Brady may be the best ever at understanding and reacting to external factors out of his direct control, such as unexpected wrinkles in what the opposing defense may be trying to do to throw him off, the state of the weather and the field, or injuries to his teammates.

This Tom Brady–like analytical approach allows a project manager to anticipate or react to changes or unexpected factors, including predicting, assessing, and mitigating risks to project performance. Again, for some this may come more naturally. This anticipation can be learned through practice to some degree, and some comes from sheer years of experience—just having seen more stuff in life.

Back to my Operation Overlord example, Eisenhower's planning was immaculate. The planning was thorough, detailed, analytical, and well practiced and included anticipating the unanticipated. D-Day was originally planned to be June 5 rather than June 6.

But early on the morning of June 5, the command center reported to Eisenhower that the weather was terrible across the English Channel. The rain, rough seas, fog, and clouds might have also surprised and disadvantaged the German forces, but after all that careful planning, readiness, and anticipation, with almost 200,000 troops, including naval vessels, air support, infantry, and logistics ready to go, Eisenhower called a one-day delay.[19]

A bit like Brady calling an audible in football, except with Operation Overlord, the stakes were a bit higher!

Eisenhower had so anticipated the many possible risks and outcomes that he had actually already written a draft memo prior to the D-Day invasion to be sent the day after D-Day if the invasion were a failure.[20] The Dwight D. Eisenhower library holds the original handwritten memo. Thankfully, he never had to send this memo, but he probably thought it best to go ahead and anticipate that possibility and what he would need to say.

Of course, there is also the famous Apollo 13 near tragedy. After exquisite training, practice, and risk scenario planning, an unexpected catastrophic accident happened on board the spacecraft. Both the astronauts in the Apollo and all the ground-based support had to figure things on the fly. They called on an amazing amount of creativity, ingenuity, and agile analytical thinking to break down the problem, brainstorm alternative solutions, weigh the risks, and select a way forward to get the Apollo back safely splashing into the ocean.

I suggest you gentlemen invent a way to put a square peg in a round hole. Rapidly.

—**Gene Kranz,** *Apollo 13* **movie**

Besides the weather or other totally external factors, in my experience, one of the key components of this analytical ability to predict, assess, and mitigate project risks is understanding the variable of human beings.

Ironically, this is not what I was taught in all my higher-level mathematics courses in undergrad or in most of my engineering management courses in grad school. But I have come to see that, as long as we still have to rely on human beings rather than computers or robots, humans will be a partly unconstrained variable (in mathematics language) in project performance. As a single factor by itself, humans' involvement in projects creates risk. And dealing with human beings puts us in the leadership realm (see Chapter 6, *People Leadership*).

The best project managers understand and can predict, assess, and mitigate the uncertainties of human involvement in projects. Humans do unpredictable things. Humans have off days and make mistakes they normally wouldn't make. Humans have highs and lows. Humans get angry at other humans and can't get along in teams to effectively execute project tasks. An analytical approach to humans means being human with them, listening with empathy, and all the other factors I have discussed in other parts of the CBL framework (especially Chapter 6). It also means looking systematically at data, trends, patterns of human behavior, and team dynamics and figuring out what each individual human needs and wants to cause them to perform.

COMMUNICATION. The final competency of project management I'll address is communication. The effective project manager must have exceptional acumen in communicating in all forms to multiple audiences. Audiences include all those with a stake in the project's success (with all of their humanness), including the customer, the project team, suppliers and subcontractors, the organization's leadership, and other external stakeholders.

Kickoff meetings, weekly or monthly status meetings, client project reviews, and other mechanisms are critical to keeping all stakeholders up to date on the project. A good communicator knows he can't just "assume" that parties are aware or up to date. The good communicator knows it is an integral part of her job to ensure that each stakeholder is up to date. And, of course, each stakeholder may require a slightly different form of communication or framing of communication. This is what I have referred to in an earlier chapter as "speaking into the listening."

As noted before, communication is not communication unless the receiver understands the message that was intended to be delivered. And communication is not communication unless the receiver has an opportunity to clarify and provide feedback.

Whether updating a client, the project team, an internal boss, or some interested third party, the project manager needs to perfect the art of clear communication and allow time and space for clarifying questions and feedback.

From a leadership lens, the project manager who is on the Complete Business Leadership path is being responsible (see my definition of being responsible in Chapter 2, *Individual Wisdom*) for the communication.

Being responsible for the communication means the leader owns whether the receiver has really gotten what was intended out of the communication. "Well, I sent the email," or "Well, I told him about the situation," is not a leadership stance. If the receiver didn't get the communication as intended, the Complete Business Leader says, "I am responsible for not causing person X to hear the communication." So the responsible leader keeps working until the receiver has the communication as it was intended. Again, a shout-out to my executive coach, Jane Smith, for helping me see communication from a responsible leader's perspective.

I have noted before how important it is to communicate early and often with clients. It is particularly important to establish a rapport **before** you have to deliver bad news or push back on evolving requirements or call a client to task for not living up to their obligations.

I experienced this even recently when I didn't get out to see a client early enough in the life of a new project and by the time I did, the project was already in crisis. It is my personal policy as a leader to go see a client in the first thirty to sixty days of a new project starting. My instincts were right to get there soon, but I just got busy and didn't go. By the time I did get out there, five months after the project started, I was working an uphill battle to establish rapport while at the same time having to respond to a failing project.

I recall another time some years ago at Futures Group when I thought I would like to visit a client project in another country. It was not long after I had taken over as CEO after leading the management buyout, and I informed one of our project directors that I was going to plan a trip out to visit the project.

By the way, one of the reasons I had thought it was time to visit the project was because I felt like the project director was not keeping me up to date on the project. The project director suggested now would not be a good time because she needed to work through a few things with the client first. As soon as she said that, it was my immediate red flag to go as soon as possible to visit. So I ignored the project director's suggestion to delay and got on a plane the next day. My "learned" instincts were right and, of course, not surprisingly, the project was in deep trouble and the client was completely unhappy.

I remember another time earlier in my career where I had established an early good rapport with the client. Later in that project, our team discovered a dangerous data breach for critical data we were maintaining on behalf of the client. I immediately let the client know, took full responsibility for it, and delivered a plan for fixing the issue so it would not happen again. Of course, they were not happy, but they were appreciative of the way we communicated quickly and clearly about it.

One of the best project communicators I have been around was my statistician colleague Rich Cohn. He had a calming way of communicating truth to all stakeholders. He communicated without hyperbole, just providing clear facts and alternatives. You never felt like he was painting over something or shunning the bad news of a project. His authentic communicating style engendered trust, no matter whether it was the client, project team, the corporation, or other partners. His style was not boisterous or aggressive but was calm, confident, and credible.

Another great project communicator I have studied is Colin Powell. He served for most of his career in active duty military, rising to the rank of four-star general and chairman of the Joint Chiefs of Staff, as the national security advisor to the president of the United States, and then as US secretary of state.

He was known for his ability to handle tremendous complexity and develop a nuanced understanding of situations, seeing the world in its shades of gray. And yet he could synthesize this complexity into clear, simple messages. I remember when the United States and its allies were planning the first Gulf War, called Operation Desert Storm, in 1991 after Iraq invaded the sovereign nation of Kuwait. When asked about the military strategy for unseating Iraq from Kuwait, General Powell said: "Our strategy to go after this army is very, very simple. First, we're going to cut it off, and then we're going to kill it." It was pretty clear and succinct!

SUMMARY COMMENTS

In this chapter I have made the case that the Complete Business Leader must be competent in the dimension of *Project Management*. Whether overseeing corporate initiatives such as launching into a new market or managing a large client project, the Complete Business Leader's project management acumen must include competencies of being organized, disciplined, analytical, and adept in communications.

The Complete Business Leader doesn't have to be the best project manager on the planet but needs to be skilled enough in these competencies to manage portfolios of projects or groups of managers who do manage projects.

In my experience, those skills are best learned by doing them—actually personally managing projects.

As a leader on the CBL journey, I will never be complete, of course, but I have found I am more credible with others I am leading since I have personally managed projects. I know firsthand what it is like to try to manage a complex multiyear project with a difficult client, unpredictable project teams, and rapidly changing external factors. This is both the challenge and thrill of project management.

Many of the technical project management skills I have highlighted above can be taught, though some aspects, such as being analytical, may come more naturally to some than others. You can even sit through the coursework and take the exams to get certified as a PMP (Professional Project Manager). I am not certified, and I don't think that getting certified automatically makes you a good project manager. But the certification does signify to the rest of the world that you have learned and practiced project management disciplines. So it certainly doesn't hurt to get certified.

I have had the challenge and honor of hands-on managing projects throughout my career, including some fascinating, impactful public health sciences projects and software development projects, though not so much anymore. I have found that those experiences helped me hone many of the other CBL dimensions, such as *People Leadership*, *Relationship Management*, and, of course, *Individual Wisdom*. So I don't think of project management as a mid-level job or a role to move past on a career ladder.

Most of us will never have the challenge, or the honor, of leading something like Operation Overlord, as General Eisenhower did. Yet the world is full of opportunity to hone our skills and cause projects to succeed.

It is not our part to master all the tides of the world, but to do what is in us for the succour of those years wherein we are set, uprooting the evil in the fields that we know, so that those who live after may have clean earth to till. What weather they shall have is not ours to rule.

—**Gandalf, J. R. R. Tolkien's *The Return of the King***

Competency	Example Behavior
Organized	o Understands and optimizes the interrelationships among schedule, cost, and quality o Effective at breaking down work into manageable, trackable elements o Is detail oriented and rigorous in tracking and organizing o Maintains project management documentation that would withstand audit o Optimizes allocation of human resources to project activities to accomplish the project
Disciplined	o Understands and can produce PERT and Gantt representations of schedules o Has working knowledge of MS Project or other project management tools o Is formally trained or certified in project management o Knowledgeable of concepts of earned value management o Has working knowledge of project cost accounting
Analytical	o Can see the big picture and grasp complexity and interdependencies of tasks, people, and processes o Shows ability to predict, assess, and mitigate risks to project performance
Communication	o Exceptional acumen in communicating in all forms to multiple types of audiences o Keeps all stakeholders up to date

BUSINESS MANAGEMENT

At the outset of my career at age twenty-three, I got a taste of how my seemingly insignificant activities and decisions in my little work group in the Westbranch building in McLean, Virginia, connected into the big company (BDM) that we were part of.

I was working on a large defense contract that had many separate task orders. At one point, the main task order I was working on was coming to the end and had no more budget. Other task orders under the same contract still had plenty of budget. A senior accountable person working on the overall contract told me I could just keep working on the scope I had been doing and charge my time to another task order with a slightly different scope that still had budget. His rationale to me was that it was all going to the same US Army client, the same overall contract, and as long as I was contributing valuable work, it was all fine. A modification had already been requested with the client to increase funding on the task order that was out of money. So I filled out my timesheet as he suggested for that pay period.

About a week later, I got a phone call to walk across the courtyard to the headquarters building because the corporate general counsel wanted to see me. I walked across the courtyard and up the elevator to the top-floor C-suite in the headquarters building of this big, faceless company that paid my paycheck. Until then, those C-suite folks were just a distant, nameless, faceless abstract concept that really didn't exist in my world.

I walked into the general counsel's palatial office. It was a massive rectangular office, lined on two sides with windows, with a big desk, a long oval table on the right, and two chairs right in front of the big desk. This conveyed power to me. Shaking and hardly able to breathe, I sat down in one of the chairs in front of the desk. The general counsel was a tall man, dressed like a classic lawyer, with a stoic face. He asked me about the task orders and my time charging. I told him what happened and wasn't sure what I had done wrong. He then educated me on the strict requirements of government contract time charging, even if it were all for the same client and delivering value for that same client. He educated me that the company's entire reputation hinged on even these seemingly small acts buried deep in the bowels of the company.

BDM was extremely entrepreneurial and gave lots of space for managers to make decisions, even fostering internal competition, but any even slight ethical misstep was a blight on the whole company. Everyone's jobs, our projects, our future ability to do the important work we were doing for our DoD clients—all were at stake.

The general counsel then let me know that, fortunately, this issue had been discovered before anything was billed to the client. And everything had been corrected. My time had been rebooked to an "unbillable" code. As a young professional who already had been pegged as high-potential talent, the company wanted to educate me, not punish me for my junior-level misunderstanding. He was clear that it was a teachable moment but could never happen again. My penance was to take a course in government contract time charging. The senior person who had told me where to charge my time was not so fortunate. He was not terminated but was relieved of his management duties.

That short visit to the general counsel's office in 1988 is still vividly etched in my memory today. A beautiful irony is that two short years later, I was working on that very same floor for the CFO's office, riding up that same elevator many times with that same general counsel. I am forever grateful to BDM and its leadership approach to teach me these early lessons and help me understand how what I did at my little desk connected to the broader business.

As I mentioned in the introduction chapter and in other places throughout this book, my first company, BDM, gave me amazing opportunities and helped shape some of the roots of the Complete Business Leader philosophy and framework. Early lessons, like the one above, helped me see the bigger business picture.

At age twenty-five, I was offered the opportunity (despite my misstep above) to leave the technical/revenue side of the company to join the corporate side of the company in the finance and accounting (F&A) group. It was a time of great change for BDM. The markets were changing. Our leadership was aging out. We were a publicly traded company, and then while I was in the corporate F&A group, we struck a deal (one of the first of its kind in our industry) with Carlyle Group to take us private. With a private equity firm invested in our company, corporate finance functions quickly took on a more pivotal role.

When I joined the F&A group on a team we called "corporate business management," I had zero formal accounting or finance training. Just before I joined, the CFO and deputy CFO left the company. A new CFO, controller, and COO were installed, all just after I joined the F&A team. A year after I joined the corporate business management team, the head of my team also left the company. The CFO looked around at who was left and, with my single year in F&A, he promoted me to run the corporate business management team. This is an example of the entrepreneurial spirit at BDM—giving people who showed promise uncommon opportunities to fulfill that promise.

Over the three years I was in the corporate F&A department, I became a dot connector. I connected dots with my F&A colleagues about the realities of winning new business and delivering projects for clients. I connected dots with project colleagues in the technical/revenue side of the business about the corporate impacts of the decisions they made on projects. I had some street cred with these folks in the operating businesses because I had lived in their world, so I was often the F&A person dispatched to talk with project leaders, business development folks, and others about corporate initiatives.

This final dimension of the CBL, called *Business Management*, brings all the pieces of Complete Business Leadership back together, delivered via an organizational vessel. If the *Individual Wisdom* dimension is the foundation of the Complete Business Leader, *Business Management* is the full outward manifestation of the Complete Business Leader that delivers value to the world through sustainable organizations.

COMPETENCIES OF BUSINESS MANAGEMENT

As with all other dimensions of the Complete Business Leader, I'll define below a set of competencies, with example characteristics or behaviors, that can be professionally developed. Many of these are interrelated or somewhat overlapping, but for simplicity I'll describe them as distinct competencies.

GOVERNANCE AND LEGAL AWARENESS. Complete Business Leaders have a solid working understanding of the legal environment that governs their industry and the geographies in which they operate. This includes knowledge on any applicable regulatory frameworks and when and how they should apply. Of course, the maze of local, provincial, national, and international laws, statutes, and ethical constructs are about as complicated as the neural networks of the human brain (well, not exactly, but attorneys seem to make a great living navigating this complexity).

No one could possibly be expected to know all of this detail. However, the Complete Business Leader must know these frameworks are there, have a healthy respect for their importance, and develop a general sense of areas of black, white, and gray.

It is not acceptable for a leader to simply claim ignorance of the legal environment in which his or her organization operates. As you can see from my introductory vignette above, when I was twenty-three and just a young professional, I learned that pretty quickly! The Complete

Business Leader must know what he knows and what he doesn't know, including knowing when to seek help from an expert.

The leader needs to also develop a working knowledge of legal and contractual agreements and documents. There are legal experts to help with the details, but ultimately the responsible leader has to know generally what is in agreements being entered into by the organization.

In my experience, leaders in larger organizations tend to know less about legal and governance matters than their counterparts in small organizations. Sometimes I have seen pretty senior leaders in large organizations be less than adequately knowledgeable and end up ceding responsibility for decisions by punting them off to attorneys.

The general counsel function should be there to provide expert legal advice in the context of the business issues and help navigate that maze of legal frameworks. The general counsel is there to help manage risk for the company, not to be the final decider. I do *not* mean that an attorney holding the general counsel role would not make a strong business leader; in fact, attorneys can make great business leaders. The wise business leader has to integrate across a range of factors, including legal and governance issues, and needs to understand enough to weigh the risks of decisions. My main point here is that the Complete Business Leader should not abdicate his responsibility to understand the legal and governance ramifications of a decision.

The work I have been involved with in the past thirteen to fourteen years involves operating internationally across many countries and legal jurisdictions. Governance frameworks in developing countries are often immature, vague, not consistently enforced, or even changing from week to week. This situation has created a fascinating learning environment. Learning how to create and lead an organization that can navigate and operate effectively across this patchwork of legal environments has been a fun challenge.

I recall a situation not long after we had sold Constella Group in late 2007 to a large public company. Our Futures Group subsidiary had an opportunity to bid and win a new contract in Afghanistan. This particular contract was not based in US or UK law; instead, the project was funded by the World Bank but the actual contract would be with the Afghan government and subject to Afghan law (such as it was at the time). And the project was to be awarded as a firm fixed price contract, meaning we would get paid a fixed amount to achieve the scope of work, regardless of how much it cost us to deliver that work.

As the head of the unit now residing inside a large parent company, I weighed the risks, sought out local counsel in Afghanistan and other advice internally, and then pressed ahead with the bid. Based on my knowledge and experience, I was confident that, despite the contract being in Afghan jurisdiction, the World Bank would be standing right beside us, holding the Afghan government's feet to the fire to ensure that they would make good use of the funds for the project and that all was above board and consistent with international contract law. It was a multimillion-dollar project that would also be implementing impactful work in Afghanistan.

Our new parent company, it turned out, had a different view. After my team bid and was awarded the project, senior officials at our parent company surprised me by directing me not to sign the contract. These officials did not understand Afghan law or what it meant to operate internationally, nor had they learned how we operated within their international subsidiary. What these officials knew was US contract law. So we stopped final negotiations on the contract.

Fortunately, at about the same time, we started the process to negotiate and implement the divestiture of Futures Group, the international subsidiary of Constella, from the public company parent. We were about to revert Futures Group to an independent company.

Incidentally, this Afghanistan situation I am describing is a good example of why the Futures Group business was not a good fit in terms of organizational ethos and why we did the divestiture in the first place.

From start to completion, we executed the management buyout transaction and divestiture in less than forty-five days, and one of my first acts as CEO of the newly independent Futures Group was to restart negotiations on the Afghan contract and ultimately sign it. The Afghan government paid part of the fixed price up front, our team implemented and managed that project (see Chapter 7, *Project Management*) flawlessly, and we got paid the entire amount of the contract on time. It turned out to be one of Futures Group's most profitable contracts ever. And, importantly, the work we did had a positive impact on the Afghan health system.

This story is not intended as a negative assessment our public company parent. They were a highly successful company with a sterling market reputation. The story is intended to demonstrate that the business leader must know enough about the legal environment to weigh the risks, with help from legal teams. The parent company senior officials didn't understand the legal environment and so were not in a position to weigh the risk properly. Furthermore, the parent company had a risk appetite that really didn't fit Futures Group's line of work and where we operated, so we were just not a good fit organizationally.

Another characteristic within governance and legal adherence is understanding what good governance looks like and applying the organization's governance and company policies. The business leader needs to be curious enough (recall Chapter 2, *Individual Wisdom*) to study and learn good governance and policy, including the rationale for these frameworks.

Every company has its own take on good governance. As the business leader takes on an increasing scope of responsibility, he or she needs to help shape or even decide on the company's governance posture. It's not acceptable for the Complete Business Leader to say, "That's the legal department's job," or to simply ignore corporate policy just because they don't like or agree with it.

However, sometimes policy does get in the way of good business, so the complete leader needs to work to change policy if necessary. This might be driven by the overall legal environment in which the organization is operating, or sometimes this is self-inflicted by the company based on its risk appetite, or even just corporate bureaucracy taking on a life of its own. Regardless, the Complete Business Leader understands, applies, and changes, if necessary, the organization's governance frameworks.

One of the most fun, challenging, and complex initiatives I drove after we completed the Futures Group management buyout (MBO) and reestablished it as an independent company was putting in place an entirely new governance framework to manage our far-flung enterprise. Over a couple year period, we studied and pieced together best practices from our previous parent companies and other market leading organizations. Given that we were reverting Futures Group to an independent company, it afforded us the opportunity to be intentional about our corporate philosophy on risk and how that should manifest in corporate governance structures. We defined and launched a governance framework with corporate, regional, and country-specific policies, standard operating procedures, tools, and templates.

The framework we implemented was so solid that when we merged Futures Group with GRM International some years later, the combined company, GRM Futures Group, adopted many of these Futures Group polices and operating procedures.

RISK MANAGEMENT. All business decisions have some amount of risk in them associated with the uncertainty of the outcome. In fact, it could be argued that any initiative or activity that is creating value not previously existing in the world must, by necessity, have an uncertain outcome and therefore have risk.

As with other aspects of the CBL framework, risk management is a well-studied and written-about topic, so I will not try to reinvent that body of work. I'll just make the case that since all business decisions have uncertainty and therefore risk, the Complete Business Leader needs to have the desire for continuous learning, curiosity, willingness to be vulnerable, and other related characteristics (see Chapter 2, *Individual Wisdom*) to effectively manage, not eliminate, risk.

When considering risk, the leader needs to understand and be able to weigh the risk/reward tradeoffs in the context of his or her organization's ethos—that is, the organization's overall mission and goals and its culture and values. External factors, including market factors or regulatory environments, come into play as well. Having a keen sense of these contextual issues is a critical component of effective risk management.

For example, something that would be viewed as extremely high risk—financially, ethically, or reputationally—for one organization might be a viewed as a minor and fully acceptable risk for another organization.

I've described in earlier chapters the way we ran Constella Group from 1999 to 2007, when we sold the company to SRA International. At Constella, we were aggressive, agile, direct, and bold and had a fairly high risk tolerance. As our lofty mission, we were trying to change the world by being a transformational force for good in global health. We took risks, made mistakes, cleaned them up, and kept moving forward at speed. This was our organizational context—our ethos—as I call it: the Complete Business Leader framework comes to life with a specific organization's ethos.

In becoming part of SRA, we became part of a large, successful public company, but one where the organizational ethos was not a match. Neither organization was right or wrong—just different. This difference proved challenging in weighing risk and making decisions. Those distinctions that made Constella great at what we did before could not flourish anymore in a different organizational context.

Specifically, in the world of managing projects, it is important to understand the business model, including risk/

reward differences for different types of contracts, such as cost reimbursable, or time and materials (fixed labor rates), or firm fixed price forms of agreement and how you get compensated in each type. It is equally as important to then be able to convey and negotiate these distinctions with clients.

Over my years in public sector outsourcing, often government clients didn't understand or fully appreciate these different risk/reward dynamics of our business model. For example, a public health client once awarded us a firm fixed price contract where we were to earn and invoice for a fixed total amount to complete an overall project. As we got toward the end of that project and were clearly going to deliver the project on time and complete the required deliverables, the client wanted to start adding scope to the work and also thought we might be making too much money. It took a lot of convincing and education to get the client to back off of his expanded demands. But clearly we, the contractor, had taken on 100 percent of the financial and performance risk, so to account for that risk we needed to have the potential of a higher return.

Another example is from the mid-1990s when I led a team at BDM to create a commercial software product as an offshoot of some work for the FDA. It was an algorithm-based machine learning software product (this is common nowadays, but in the late 1990s, it was groundbreaking) to improve categorization of clinical information.

My team and I negotiated a Cooperative Research and Development Agreement with the FDA, which allowed us to add on to the work we had already completed for FDA and create a commercially viable product. FDA was to receive a royalty back for every license sold. We created a business plan to sell these licenses and accompanying consulting services packages. Because a commercial software product business was not the norm at BDM, we had to do some convincing of our own company's executive management of the necessary up-front investment and time horizon for recouping our investment and making money. We also had to obtain FDA's concurrence in the licensing and associated pricing models. In order to make it financially viable, the gross margins on license sales had to be 75 percent or more.

There was a substantial R&D investment plus marketing and other general administrative costs required. Helping FDA and our own executives, of course, required in-depth understanding of the risks and being able to convey the commercial rationale. Investing well in advance of sales or cash flows was a new model with an entirely different risk profile for our company, which was geared primarily to government contracting services.

FINANCIAL ACUMEN. The Complete Business Leader does not have to be a certified public accountant or have a finance degree, but he or she must understand and be able to make sound business decisions based on a range of accounting and financial factors. Without the finance or accounting degree, having an analytically trained mind helps. Having a questioning, inquisitive, organized mind-set is critical.

It is important to at least understand accounting processes at a conceptual level—particularly why accountants do what they do. For example, understanding best accounting approaches to accruals, what might be accrued and not accrued, helps the business leader assess and understand where the project or business unit or overall company is financially.

In my three years in corporate F&A at BDM, I got a crash on-the-job coursework. I learned the basics of accounting debits and credits all the way to understanding dynamics of optimizing cash flow and balancing corporate debt with growth. My boss also drilled into me the disciplines of documenting and annotating my financial analyses, including how to check and cross-check my financial reports.

After my three years in corporate finance, I moved back into the technical/revenue part of BDM. Subsequently, because of my project and corporate experience, I was periodically brought back in to help on corporate finance initiatives.

For example, when BDM acquired a sizable German company in 1993, I was asked to spend a few weeks in Germany helping on integration. One of the key things I focused on was how they managed projects financially, including revenue recognition, application of corporate overheads, and project cost accounting as part of their job cost system. My work also included modeling out what the combined company should look like in terms of functions and operating expenses and where we could gain operational efficiencies.

In the course of my integration work, I studied the German company's accounting processes and procedures and learned there is some truth to the adage that Germans make great accountants. Their systems, approaches, and files were something we could learn from as the acquirer. Besides eating amazing German food and drinking the best beer I have ever had, it was a totally awesome learning experience!

I also jumped at the opportunity to work on a major financial system migration when BDM moved from its old mainframe-based system to SAP's enterprise resource planning (ERP) system. As a large government services contractor, we were one of the early adopters of SAP, though it required significant customization for our government services business. I spent about a year loaned out on planning and implementation teams while still running my own projects, again helping to connect dots between corporate accounting and finance requirements and the needs of project managers from the SAP system.

These were both tremendous experiences for me where I continued to solidify my own finance understanding and contributed to important corporate initiatives.

The Complete Business Leader needs to understand the relationship between project-level financials and how they roll up to and impact corporate financial success. Sometimes optimizing on a particular project and its success can be suboptimal for the rolled-up corporate financials.

For example, it might be ideal on an individual project to slow down the financial burn rate or delay a project milestone to a later reporting period. This might be because the client wants it that way or because the project team needs to focus on another aspect of the project. Yet these decisions may negatively impact the financial results of the company, particularly if the project is a large one. The Complete Business Leader has to find a way to optimize the project (*Project Management*), the client relationship (*Relationship Management*), the people involved (*People Leadership*), *and* the company's financial performance (*Business Management*).

The Complete Business Leader certainly needs to be comfortable reviewing basic financial statements of income statement, balance sheet, and cash flow and have a conceptual understanding of the interrelated nature of these. It is important to grasp how revenue on an income statement becomes cash (hopefully) on a cash flow statement and how cash ties into assets on the balance sheet. What is more important is to know what to *do* with this information. Being able to interpret current financial statements and influence future financial performance with the decisions of today are important learned skills.

These skills become critical when trying to assess, for example, an M&A transaction and convince your private equity partner why a deal should be done. As I have mentioned previously, at Constella Group we brought in a private equity partner in 2004 for a minority stake in our company. We did this because we needed access to more capital to grow aggressively.

Bringing in private equity partners changed the dynamic of our decision making and ultimately the trajectory of our company. We didn't always agree with our private equity board members, but our whole leadership team learned a tremendous amount in a few short years, including learning how much we didn't know! We argued with them over deals and growth strategies and, of course, operating expenses, and together we made Constella a better company by almost every measure.

Having a private equity partner is not for everyone, but in the Constella Group case it made us better and more valuable. Our private equity partner's sole focus was increased shareholder value. As inspirational as our company's mission was for the management team, for the private equity team the mission was a means to an end: increasing shareholder value.

Among other things, the private equity partners helped our management team learn how to unemotionally and analytically evaluate strategic investments and their relationship to value creation, how to rigorously go about due diligence, how to question ourselves and our assumptions, and how to effectively make and defend our case for the strategic direction of the organization.

Truthfully, there was some pain for me in the way we began to run the company increasingly focused on shareholder value. Yet at the end when we sold the company, we had certainly created financial success for the shareholders of Constella Group, including me. I would have loved to have been able to pull together the financing to be the buyer and keep running Constella as an independent company, but the reality is we had created such a valuable business that it was way too expensive.

However, I stayed in touch with one of the private equity partners (see also Chapter 3, *Relationship Management*), and a year later, he was instrumental in helping structure the deal to divest Futures Group (the MBO I have referred to) subsidiary. And when I ventured out on my own in 2015, that same private equity partner provided regular counsel to me that was candid and helpful, and it was also willing to invest in me as an individual entrepreneur.

Another example of how these interrelationships of project-level revenues, costs, billing, and collections become more than a textbook exercise is working capital. I understood working capital intellectually, but I *really* internalized it deep in my bones shortly after we did the Futures Group MBO.

We divested Futures Group from the large public company parent in September 2008, just as the global financial system was seizing up. For a variety of reasons, in the MBO transaction we didn't negotiate an adequate amount of working capital. Within forty-five days after the divestiture, my CFO and I were in near panic mode, wondering how much longer we would be able to make payroll. Our government contracting receivables were reliable to be paid eventually, but we didn't have enough cash to meet our near-term cash obligations—most important, payroll. Under normal times, we would have had no problem getting a standard bank line of credit for working capital on reasonable terms, given our client receivables. However, we were considered risky as a new organization having just completed the MBO, and by the fall of 2008, traditional banks had basically stopped lending money.

This raw fear moved my CFO and me to action quickly. We made some aggressive moves to pull cash back from our thirty-plus country operations and then tightly control how we funded our foreign bank accounts, we stretched out other payments, we went to our clients to try to collect quicker, and we accelerated billing and moved to twice per month rather than monthly invoicing. We also explored more exotic financial instruments and institutions, including factoring companies and mezzanine debt.

Fortunately, with the actions we took above, we eked out just enough cash to get through a scary five-month period and by early 2009 were generating enough cash to fund our own operations. Later, after we really didn't need it anymore, we were able to secure a working capital line of credit through a traditional banking institution, as well as refinance the debt we took on as part of the MBO, on friendly lending terms.

From this experience, I learned—up close and personal—that cash really is king in business, and my financial acumen came in handy. And this is not just about for-profit businesses making profits. Whether a startup health tech company, a church, or other large nonprofit, the business management requirements around cash are the same. Over multiple periods, you must get more cash in the door than goes out.

STRATEGIC PERSPECTIVE. Complete Business Leaders can see and process at multiple layers, from fine levels of detail to broad trends and everything in between. And Complete Business Leaders can analyze, process, and make decisions based on nonlinear inputs. In my experience, Complete Business Leaders see the world through a 3-D lens of networks and interrelationships rather than thinking linearly. This allows complete leaders to have a *strategic perspective.*

This strategic perspective includes being able to grasp and apply the organization's business model— fundamentally, how the organization creates value and how it gets paid to create that value.

For most of my career, the business model I have operated in involves pulling together the knowledge of experts to deliver project results and getting paid to deliver the people, the result, or some combination. The payment has usually come in the form of getting paid by the hour or day, though increasingly clients are interested in paying a fixed amount for a project result.

As I mentioned just above, I did have the opportunity to learn and build out a new business model in the mid-1990s when I led the creation of a medical terminology matching software product to be sold to the pharmaceutical industry. In this model, we charged a licensing fee plus an annual maintenance fee. This was a great learning experience for me, including the challenge of how to convince others in the company of the viability of this new business model.

The Complete Business Leader also articulates corporate strategy and can map the linkages (or networked relationships) to his or her team's work. For example, there might be an overarching strategic approach to developing talent. The individual business leader must be able to convey that strategic approach to his own teams and integrate that approach to talent development into his own team's strategy and scope.

For example, Shannon Hader, my colleague from Futures Group, had mastery of articulating the organization's strategy and linking that to her team's work and to their execution of the strategy. Until she came to Futures Group, Shannon had never worked in a for-profit company before. She had worked in government and academia. Yet she had a broad integrative view—the strategic perspective—and she quickly figured out the dynamics of our organization, including our business model and the similarities and differences between our organization's ethos and previous organizations she had worked for.

Shannon then translated our strategy into action. She was able to get her teams reorganized and refocused on our goals. For example, though Shannon had previously worked in organizational constructs that didn't have financial incentives (such as bonuses and stock options), she quickly figured out how to use these new tools to align her team's execution to our strategy.

Another example of this characteristic is my old colleague John Cook. I referred to John in earlier chapters about *Relationship Management*. In addition to his well-honed relationship management competency, John was also a very strategic thinker. John helped teach me the art of taking the "long view"—that is, making short-term or micro decisions always with the long term in mind. This also means sometimes sacrificing short-term results in favor of the long view. No matter how small or seemingly insignificant the decision, John always asked me what we were trying to achieve long term and how my decision might fit into the overall company direction.

One of the advanced practices we learned and applied at Constella Group was strategic alignment: developing long-term goals and strategies and aligning all decisions, operations, people, and processes around achieving the long-term. With some outside consulting help, we applied a variant of the world-renowned Balanced Scorecard methodology[21] developed by Kaplan and Norton.

Many organizations tend to apply a very linear, sequential approach to the Balanced Scorecard; however, at Constella we applied an approach that involved defining a network of interrelated strategies and goals captured on a strategy map, ultimately leading to achievement of value creation for the world and our shareholders. We had annual planning cycles and cascaded strategic alignment deep into the organization, and we reassessed and realigned every quarter. Our strategies across the key dimensions of the Balanced Scorecard were interrelated and tied together through metrics. Over several years of practice, we honed our own Constella way of applying these strategic approaches.

One of the most important skills our Constella Group leadership team became increasingly better at was how we communicated that strategy across our diverse organization and achieved clear alignment across all work groups, departments, units, and geographies. As our enterprise became increasingly spread around the world, it was a tremendous challenge to clearly articulate corporate strategy and create alignment at all levels in order to execute on the strategy. In cascading alignment, we had to take into account how the strategic language would land in different languages, cultures, educational backgrounds, and interests across our employee population. The strategic messaging had to be clean, simple, and succinct and inspire action.

A final characteristic of the strategic perspective is when the Complete Business Leader makes sound, holistic business decisions by weighing many factors. These factors include considering corporate risk and client, project, people, and financial impacts and integrating across both short-term requirements and long-term goals. The Complete Business Leader optimizes for the best overall business decision with this strategic perspective lens. This requires understanding the interrelatedness of many factors.

For example, choosing to take on corporate debt to complete an acquisition not only creates a direct financial risk/ reward for the company but also influences and sometimes transforms other factors as well. This debt may change the nature of relationships with clients or other external partners. It may affect how the company goes about making decisions and achieving all its other goals, how management deals with its board and shareholders, how it operates current projects, or how pays its people. Debt can change the very core ethos of the company. In short, what might seem like primarily a financial ROI decision is really an integrated business decision—one that the Complete Business Leader with a strategic perspective is positioned to make.

My colleague and friend Alonzo Fulgham spent most of his career as a public servant before moving out into the private sector. For many, even at executive levels in government as Alonzo was, this transition into the private sector is difficult. The strategic perspective in government often does not include blending risk with long-term strategy, people, capital allocation, and measurement of value creation. Alonzo, on the other hand, from the first time I met him as he was retiring from government, had that ability to see multidimensionally, to assess and weigh multiple complex factors affecting value creation.

Serving on my board at Futures Group, Alonzo frequently and effectively challenged my team and me to consider new markets, new business models, and new strategic approaches to achieve our goals. He was able to challenge us in ways that inspired us to think differently while still giving us the space to manage the company day to day.

The CEO of DAI, where I am currently building out a new global health business, is one of the best I have experienced at this strategic perspective competency. As I mentioned in Chapter 6, Jim Boomgard has street cred in our industry and within our company because he has pretty much done every job there is to do in the company, including running field programs in Indonesia for ten years.

In a discussion with Jim, you can tell that he is continuously processing in his head all of the delicate and sometimes nuanced interrelationships among a range of factors in any business situation. Some of this is just pure experience, and some of this is how he has trained his curious mind to process and weigh inputs, map complexity, see all the interconnections in 3-D, and take the long view—all examples of the strategic perspective.

SUMMARY COMMENTS

In this chapter, I described four key competencies involved in the *Business Management* dimension of the Complete Business Leader: governance and legal awareness, risk management, financial acumen, and strategic perspective.

Some of the competencies in this *Business Management* dimension may sound like corporate things (legal, risk, finance, strategy) that a mid-level manager has limited ability to consider. I stipulate, however, that even if a leader is not in a position today to directly make a lot of these kinds of decisions, he or she should still be learning and considering all of these factors in all decisions.

Referring back to my colleague and friend John Cook: he pushed me to consider the long view in every small, seemingly minor decision and helped me be a more Complete Business Leader. And back to the story I began this chapter with, at BDM I got my first lesson at twenty-three that the seemingly small and insignificant decisions I made had potentially far-reaching and multidimensional impacts on BDM's business.

These competencies are what help the business leader not only be complete intellectually but use that completeness in practice to deliver value to the world through an organizational vessel. The *Business Management* dimension, like all others in the CBL, is never finished. As the leader comes to mastery of business management, there is a realization that more can always be learned.

As I've progressed in my career, I've come to appreciate—and really value—the other attributes that define a company's success beyond the P&L: great leadership, long-term financial strength, ethical business practices, evolving business strategies, sound governance, powerful brands, values-based decision making.

—Ursula Burns, former CEO of Xerox

Competency	Example Behavior
Governance and legal awareness	o Has knowledge of relevant regulations o Has a working knowledge of legal/contractual agreements and documents o Understands and applies good governance and company policies o Knows when to seek expert legal advice
Risk management	o Understands different contract types and their relationship to company and project-level risk o Understands company business processes and roles and when and to whom to raise issues o Understands and weighs risk/reward tradeoffs
Financial acumen	o Understands relationship between project financials and corporate financials o Understands concepts of sound accounting processes, including separation of duties o Understands overheads and their application o Reads and understands income statement, balance sheet, and cash flow statements o Understands the relationship of project costs, revenue recognition, billing, and collections
Strategic perspective	o Understands and applies the organization's business model o Articulates corporate strategy and how their work maps to the strategy o Makes sound, holistic business decisions; weighs all factors, including corporate risk, client relationship, project performance, and people issues and impacts o "Sees" multidimensionally

09

COMPLETE BUSINESS
LEADER IN ACTION

Written by Liz Mallas

A few years ago, one of the members of Chris's executive team, Shannon Hader, who is mentioned earlier in this book, walked into my office at Futures Group and asked how I would feel about moving to Swaziland. Not long after—maybe just a couple of weeks—my bags were packed and I was moving to Swaziland to run a large government-funded project that was not performing.

Chris visited a few weeks after my arrival and sat through one of my always very tense team-lead meetings. There weren't enough chairs at our large conference table because the group was about twenty people, so Chris sat behind me—almost directly behind me. Tensions were high in this meeting because of a historical lack of communication and performance. This tension spilled into our conversations as we went through our agenda items. As the brand new lead of this team, I was under a lot of pressure to turn this project around. And in this meeting, I felt that pressure even more intimately with Chris sitting right behind me. At the end of that meeting, Chris said something to me that has stuck with me since: he said he would have run the meeting exactly as I did. His words helped shore up the confidence I needed to lead that team through some substantial change. We went from a team that was struggling to one that was performing.

I owe a lot of what I was able to do with that team and the project to the model I saw and was guided by in Chris and his executive team. Nearly *all* of them came to visit me in Swaziland, sometimes multiple times. They set and then modeled the culture for Futures Group, which, as you'll read toward the end of this chapter, is incredibly important when being intentional about growing CBL dimensions in your teams.

Before being offered the opportunity to move to Swaziland, I worked for Futures Group in many different capacities for almost seven years, having started as an intern in our Mexico City office. As he said in a previous chapter, Chris fully believes in giving people uncommon opportunities—positions that will really grow you professionally and personally. My first foray in our Mexico City office was an uncommon opportunity; while he's not the one who gave it to me, those kinds of opportunities were a huge piece of the culture of Futures Group. As a midsize business, individuals often had multiple responsibilities across a variety of disciplines and had to learn to sink or swim. That learning taught so many life lessons.

After Swaziland and a short stint in South Africa, I transitioned to our London office (and later to North Carolina)—another one of those uncommon opportunities. Chris and I began working together to build a program around the Complete Business Leader framework. I was in the middle of completing a master of organization development degree, and he was in the middle of managing a cultural integration between Futures Group and the company we had merged with, GRM International, a year prior. We needed a program to bring the two companies together, identify top talent, and support that talent in realizing their incompleteness so that they could begin a pilgrimage to completeness.

As Chris might say, we wanted to intentionally and systematically develop a bunch of Gandalfs. I've never seen any of the Lord of the Rings movies in its entirety—don't tell Chris. So while all of this was going on, I needed a capstone project to finish out my masters. The no-brainer was to do something with the Complete Business Leader program.

As you'll read later in this chapter, I designed and implemented an evaluation of our Gandalf-building initiative. We wanted to learn more about the best ways to implement a program. I dove into the literature and used it to build on what Chris had started years before. We tailored approaches and used best practices. This chapter is a summary of what we learned through that process.

After the Futures Group MBO in 2008, Chris began rolling out the new standalone company's organizational ethos and its strategy, policies, and procedures. During this rollout, Chris started presenting and integrating different aspects of this "complete leader" competency model that he had been working on. Chris and his leadership team were setting the culture of our newly independent organization, and Chris knew that sharing his ideas around these dimensions was a big part of setting that culture. In order to matter and impact culture, the values of an organization need to be espoused and modeled. Integrating the CBL framework did both.

Later, after the merger with GRM, we went through another process of setting strategy using the Balanced Scorecard[22] approach, and refining policies and procedures. Again, the now-named Complete Business Leader framework was integrated into the company-wide cascading communications as a way to set expectations and inform the culture of the organization.

Meanwhile, we began building out and implementing the CBL Program—a program that would orient our top talent to the framework, help them become more self-aware in the CBL dimensions, and give them opportunities (didactic, experiential, and reflection) to develop those dimensions. Sometimes it was like building a plane while flying it too, but it worked. We did baseline and midline 360-degree feedback[23] assessments that mapped to the seven CBL dimensions to help the selected cohort get to know themselves better and to develop an individualized plan to address the gaps revealed in the feedback and ratings. The assessments also served as a way to know whether there was a change in our CBLers (as we called them) over a period of time.

The CBLers were a cohort of seven mid-level individuals who had submitted applications to be considered for the CBL program and were subsequently chosen to participate by the merged company's executive team. The cohort represented mid-levels from all of our major office locations: DC, London, Brisbane, Pretoria, and Dubai.

Based on the feedback from the assessments, which were tailored to provide the CBLers feedback on their abilities in each of the seven CBL dimensions, the cohort members created individualized development plans that included executive coaching, mentoring, networking, stretch job assignments, action learning, and lots and lots of reflection. I'm sure all of the CBLers got really used to my many open-ended questions and awkward pauses as I waited for them to respond. The program development was informed by the literature and research in leadership development, all aligned to the CBL framework.

The evaluation of the program itself was also informed by the literature and research. I'll describe more about the evaluation and the change in the participants later in the chapter. Here's how our lab experiment went.

CBL PROGRAM IMPLEMENTATION

To start the program, each of the seven CBLers completed the WorkPlace Big Five profile (a workplace personality assessment) and the WorkPlace Performance 360 assessment at the beginning of the program. Both of these instruments provided feedback around human resource optimization, specific to the CBL seven dimensions. For the 360 assessment, the CBLer asked a minimum of fifteen respondents—including their direct supervisor, matrixed supervisors, peers, direct reports, and field-level representatives—to provide feedback on questions related to the CBL dimensions. Participants were then taught how to understand their results so they could see where their energy is (or is not) for these dimensions and where they are (or are not) performing.

This information served as the basis for their Individual Leadership Development Plan, whereby each participant had to outline, based on their data, how they would develop each CBL dimension. Participants were given a small budget for outside consultants and trainings. Each CBLer was assigned an internal mentor and an external executive coach, participated in two in-person leadership development workshops (which included multiple opportunities for sharing information and networking), worked as part of a cohort to address a real challenge that the business was facing (an action learning cohort challenge), and was assigned stretch assignments that manifested as job roles in the merged company's strategy execution process.

A year later, a second 360 was administered to document change in performance over that period. Again, a minimum of fifteen individuals per CBL participant were asked to respond to the WorkPlace Performance 360 survey, using the same categories of responders as the first. CBLers were expected to update their development plans with input from this second round of feedback.

We began this program with the assumption that an intervention can change an individual, consistent with Chris's premise in the introduction of this book that you can grow and transform yourself as a leader. The intervention might be in the learning, growth, or change in how an individual thinks about something, but the assumption is that change will occur.[24] As I mentioned, diving into the literature to inform our program development was important to us so that we were using best practice approaches.

What I learned is that *leader development* and *leadership development* are not synonymous terms. *Leader development* focuses on the development of the individual, specifically their personal power, knowledge, and trustworthiness, while *leadership development* focuses on social capital and development of relationships through commitments, mutual respect, and trust.[25] *Leader development* focuses on how effective an individual is in their roles and processes, within the leadership context, through a variety of developmental experiences. *Leader development* is individual development. *Leadership development* is collective development. The development of leaders and of leadership are two separate processes, but they are not mutually exclusive. To be transparent, in the development and implementation of this program, we were trying to accomplish both—*leader* and *leadership development.* This meant that we had to combine approaches of both *leader* and *leadership development*, so I looked for the best practices of both.

There are many different ways to grow these dimensions in your team members and in yourself. However, we've learned in reading the research and in experience that a multi-activity approach that includes didactic learning, experiential learning, and reflection has the best results for both *leader* and *leadership development.* Individuals grow when you take them outside of their comfort zone, so you have to figure out how to get them (and yourself) there and then grow.

As I've mentioned, our approach was informed by research and literature. The evaluation, which will be outlined in the next section, was heavily informed by Kirkpatrick's four levels for evaluating training programs (more on that soon). The program development was informed by many different sources, but I found this summary written by D. V. Day to be the most concise when understanding how—and why—to incorporate a multi-activity approach that is didactic, experiential, and reflective. The summary presents six impactful leadership development practices with the reasons for the implementation, including the strengths and weaknesses of using them. See below.

Day's Summary of Selected Practices in Leadership Development[26]

Practice	Descriptions	Development Target	Strengths	Weaknesses
360-degree feedback	Multi-source ratings of performance, organized and presented to an individual	Self-knowledge; Behavorial change	Comprehensive picture; broad participation	Overwhelming amount of data; no guidance on how to change; time and effort
Coaching	Practical, goal-focused form of one-on-one learning	Self-knowledge; Behavorial change; Career development	Personlized incentive	Perceived stigma (remedial); expensive
Mentoring	Advising/ develomental relationship, usually with a more senior manager	Broader understanding; Advancement catalyst; Lessons learned/avoid mistakes	Strong personal bond	Peer jealousy; over-dependence
Networks	Connecting to others in different functions and areas	Better problem-solving; Learning who to consult for project help	Builds organization	Ad hoc; unstructured
Job assignments	Providing "stretch" assignment in terms of role, function, or geography	Skill development; Broader understanding of the business	Job relevant; accelerates learning	Conflict between performance and development; no structure for learning
Action learning	Project-based learning directed at important business problems	Socialization; Teamwork; Implement strategy	Tied to business imperatives; action oriented	Time intensive; leadership lessons not always clear overemphasis on results.

CBL PROGRAM EVALUATION

Going into this, we structured the program so we would be able to identify any improvement in participants' performance in the CBL dimensions. We also wanted to know what components of the program were most helpful in that development. As we were building the plane and flying it, we were also fidgeting with its flying mechanisms. We developed an explanatory sequential mixed-method evaluation framework so that we would know the answers to these questions.

To inform the design of the evaluation, I looked into the literature on training program evaluation. Kirkpatrick[27] offers a simple model for evaluating training programs that has become the foundational model for thinking through this body of knowledge. Kirkpatrick's model includes four steps.

The first step is reaction, whereby a training evaluator needs to know whether or not the trainees liked a particular program. The second step is learning, which is a measure of the knowledge gained, skills gained or improved, and/ or attitudes that changed as a result of the training. The third step is behavior, which is a measure of how much participants' behavior changes as a result of the training. And finally, the fourth step is results, which is a measure of whether or not the desired results of the training were achieved.

So here's how we used that model to understand our own program.

To understand the change in performance over the time period (steps two and three in Kirkpatrick's model),

I analyzed the data from the 360 assessments, with the participants' consent. The data was anonymized so that I could analyze the information objectively. I looked at the change in the responses to the 360 assessment questions from baseline to midline to identify performance improvements or declines in CBL dimensions. I also looked at whether an individual's self-reported scores changed from baseline to midline in each dimension, and if so, whether the gap between the self-report and rater evaluations increased or decreased. The gap between the self-report number versus all-other-raters report number served as a guide for understanding the CBLers perceived performance compared to performance as defined and averaged by all-other-raters.

Each of the dimensions that was measured (*Individual Wisdom, Relationship Management, Thought Leadership, Business Growth, People Leadership, Project Management,* and *Business Management*) had competencies. These competencies were weighted differently based on the definition of the CBL dimension to give a final score. To come to a conclusion about whether or not there was an "overall improvement" in the CBL dimensions, the final scores for each individual were added and an average was found.

A more sophisticated and time-intensive analysis could have been to look at each individual's self and rater responses and develop an algorithm that would have more closely examined whether CBL participant performance improved or not. But I didn't do this. We just used an average. It's a limitation of this analysis, and it's not the only one. While literature-informed, the study wasn't perfect.

In addition to the 360 performance review quantitative data, I also implemented a semi-structured interview with the program participants, their supervisors, and their mentors about which program components were least supportive, whether or not the respondent thought the program had created any business impact, and what recommendations they would make for the program in the future (Kirkpatrick steps one and four). These interviews were recorded, transcribed, and then coded by a research assistant and me—again in an anonymized manner so the identity of the participant did not impact the analysis.

CBL PROGRAM IMPACT

Overall, we observed an improvement in performance in the CBL dimensions. This group of leaders all moved further into their pilgrimage of completeness through their participation in this program. Goal achieved!

However, improvement was uneven. While every CBLer improved their performance, there wasn't improvement in every single person, in every single dimension. When averaging the feedback, we found that there was an improvement in only six of the seven CBL dimensions. The largest gains in performance were found in *Business Growth, Business Management,* and *Thought Leadership.* The smallest gains in performance were found in *People Leadership* and *Project Management.* Although the overall score for CBL competencies did not show large changes, the change in competencies varied widely in both positive and negative directions.

We found that there was a general consensus (almost unanimous) that there was positive business impact as a result of the CBL program. This means that the participants and executives serving in the roles of mentors and supervisors thought the program added value to the business. Through the qualitative analysis, we also found that the most helpful components for the CBLers' development were the 360 assessment feedback, executive coaching, and the action learning cohort challenge.

We were somewhat surprised that the program didn't seem to improve the self-awareness of the program participants. This was measured in the change in the average of the gap between self-report numbers and all-other-rater report numbers over the time period. I've thought a lot about this, and I think it's mostly a reflection on where the organization was at that point in time. More on this later.

And that CBL dimension that didn't improve overall? It was *Individual Wisdom*. In the summary diagram that Chris provides in the next chapter, you'll note that *Individual Wisdom* is connected to all other dimensions. And yet all other dimensions improved across the group. As Chris has mentioned, *Individual Wisdom* is foundational to all other dimensions. Had we seen an improvement in *Individual Wisdom*, we likely would have seen a larger improvement in the other six dimensions. But we didn't. And I think most of it has to do in the timing and culture of the organization when we were implementing this "lab experiment." Again, more on this later.

To further understand the relationship between these dimensions, I completed a correlation analysis. While most regressions showed little significance in correlation, there were high correlations between *Business Management* and *People Leadership*, *Business Management* and *Project Management*, and *People Leadership* and *Project*

Management. This validated Chris's model—at least at the top. Chris's diagram in Chapter 10 is a visualization of these correlations.

OK, so back to that culture I mentioned at the start of this chapter. While completing this master's program, I became a junkie of Schein, the workplace culture guru. Schein defines culture as "a pattern of shared basic assumptions learned by a group as it solved its problems of external adaptation and internal integration." The culture of this merged organization was one of a lot of change and moving parts. The dust had not settled from the merger before the program began and ended. In addition, there were other acquisitions along the way. In a large organization with a dominant culture, this likely would not have mattered.

However, as I previously mentioned, this program was being used to set the culture course for the merged organization. The CBL program got a little ahead of itself. With so many moving people and pieces, there was no dominant culture. Chris had transitioned out of his role within the organization during the latter part of CBL program implementation and was doing the external consulting that he mentioned in a previous chapter. And while I remained, there were quite a few new players to the scene during the program implementation.

As mentioned, the largest gains in improvement were demonstrated in *Business Growth* and *Business Management,* which were the two espoused priorities of this merged company. Senior leadership modeled behaviors in these two dimensions extremely well. The general awareness within the company and the CBL program participants of these priorities (and seeing them modeled) could explain the large improvements in these two dimensions. Many of the Individual Leadership Development Plans focused on these two dimensions. In addition, these two dimensions were extremely well resourced in the company as a whole. There was a large focus during this period on proposal writing (*Business Growth*) and operations efficiency (*Business Management*).

What a company prioritizes, it resources. The budget follows a company's values. Had different focus and resource priorities been given to other dimensions, there might have been more improvement across the dimensions.

The organizational ethos was being refined through this intense year of change for the company. The organization lost several senior leaders, acquired a management consulting firm, developed a strategy and strategy execution plan, rebranded, and simultaneously reorganized under a different senior leadership team and different structure.

The growth in the company was phenomenal. It was an incredibly exciting period. That season laid the groundwork for subsequent significant positive impact on the company. Change was happening faster than culture could be set. Given the aforementioned fluid culture, the refining organizational ethos, and the overall change, the structural supports for leader and leadership development were not as optimal as they could have been during the program implementation.

Back to Schein: the culture of the organization must support the Complete Business Leader framework. If it doesn't, that doesn't mean that there can't be Complete Business Leaders within the organization. On the contrary, being a Complete Business Leader can happen despite the environment in which an individual works.

However, if the organization wants to promote the framework and get behind the development of these dimensions in their talent, then they must model it from the top down. The seven dimensions of the CBL need to be embedded into the values and lifeblood of the organization. Culture can have a significant impact on an organization's overall performance. An organization with a set, defined, and stable culture that helps anticipate and adapt to change will be associated with superior performance over longer periods of time.

As companies become global, grow in size, and experience change, the need for strong leaders grows. Culture is likely to become an even more important factor in the future to determine an organization's success or failure. A Complete Business Leader approach can help drive greater effectiveness within a company experiencing these changes. To have maximum impact, the culture of an organization must be open to leader and leadership development and growth and provide the structure for doing so.

The CBL program was impactful to the individuals who participated in it and to the business. Small improvements multiply when observed by multiple individuals at a senior level. This impact can be even further multiplied when a CBL program is implemented at the right time for the organization.

10

CONCLUDING THOUGHTS

A Commander-in-Chief . . . must be self-effacing, quick to give credit, ready to
meet the other fellow more than half way, must seek and absorb advice and must
learn to decentralize. On the other hand, when the time comes that he feels he
must make a decision, he must make it in a clean-cut fashion and on his own
responsibility and take full blame for anything that goes wrong.
—**Dwight D. Eisenhower, quoted in Jean Edward Smith's _Eisenhower in War and Peace_**

From his graduation at West Point in 1915 until March 1941, almost twenty-six years, Dwight Eisenhower crawled up the officer ranks to lieutenant colonel. From March 1941, when he was promoted to full colonel, he blasted ahead to five-star general in just four years.[28] This quick progression was partly the due to the times he lived in. With the sovereignty of nations and the freedom of the world on the line, many career military officers were called on to take on much bigger roles than they had had previously. Some were not up to the task, but Eisenhower had readied himself for that moment. Eisenhower was nominated to serve as supreme commander of the Allied forces in Europe and lead Operation Overlord not because he was the single best field commander, or the single best strategist, or the world's best logistics planner, or the most beloved people person. He was selected because he was the most complete.

And this is the premise of my book and the Complete Business Leader framework: *Organizations of any size and focus will have bigger impact and be more successful by any measure when its leaders are well rounded and grounded, can integrate across disciplines, and can inspire diverse followers to produce results.*

Eisenhower was not a perfect leader. I have yet to study or experience one. According to biographers, Eisenhower could sometimes be aloof, sometimes hold a grudge, sometimes didn't apply his usual situational awareness and good judgment of people.[29] He made some bad field decisions in completing the defeat of the Germans after D-Day invasion that arguably prolonged the war in Europe possibly by months.[30] While on his watch as president of the United States, our intelligence operatives facilitated the overthrow of at least two sovereign governments (Iran, Guatemala)[31]. So no leader should be placed on a pedestal so high that the leader can no longer see the ground.

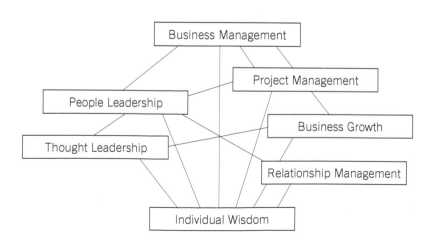

I use Eisenhower as a closing example, though, because he exemplifies the interconnected nature of the seven dimensions of the Complete Business Leader framework. His *Relationship Management* capability directly connected to his *People Leadership* and *Project Management* competency. And he became more effective in people leadership after he, late in his career, gained credibility and expertise as a field commander (*Thought Leadership*). And while he may not have needed to read a balance sheet in the European Theater (that came later in his career, by the way), he had developed a fundamental understanding of the *Business Management* of war—he knew the costs and benefits of his decisions, including the political, financial, and human tradeoffs.

After Eisenhower returned from Europe, he was made president of Columbia University. There he leveraged his relationship management acumen to "grow the business." Columbia raked in significant additional donations, prestige, and acclaim. And he leveraged several dimensions in effectively managing the business of Columbia University. For example, according to Jean Edward Smith's *Eisenhower in War and Peace,* on Eisenhower's watch Columbia finally balanced its budget.[32]

And all other dimensions of leadership were grounded in his individual wisdom—Eisenhower knew himself, who he was. He was:

- o Organized – He spent his time on highest value items and decisions.
- o Curious – He asked lots of questions of his teams without presuming to know the answers.

- o Continuous learning – He made mistakes but learned from them, as in the WWII North Africa campaign.
- o Cool under pressure – He carried the weight of the free world on his shoulders leading up to D-Day and was likely highly stressed but conveyed calm and confidence to his political bosses, commanders, and field troops.
- o Courageous – He made the hard calls and decisions, knowing the risk and what was at stake.
- o Responsible – He was always clear that the final decisions and consequences of those decisions rested with him.

That *Individual Wisdom*, as manifested in other dimensions of the Complete Business Leader, was on full display during his eight years as president of the United States, a time of economic prosperity, US infrastructure building, advances in science and education, and relative world peace compared to the previous decade.

While Eisenhower comes closest, no leader I have seen is the Complete Business Leader. There are, however, archetypes for each of the seven CBL dimensions I highlight in the table below that might help complete the illumination of what I mean. The "archetype" means this person epitomizes, or personifies, a particular dimension of the Complete Business Leader. One column represents a universally recognized name, and the next column highlights a leader I have personally known (who mostly likely is not a household name to you). My own career journey, as well as my development of the CBL framework, have been influenced by the archetype leaders I list below. The leaders I have worked with are also all mentioned elsewhere in the book.

Dimension	Archetype (household names)	Archetype (leaders I have worked with)
Business Management	Jack Welch	Jim Boomgard CEO of DAI Global
Project Management	Dwight D. Eisenhower	Frank Wilkinson An early boss at BDM in health IT
People Leadership	Dabo Swinney	Rich Podurgal Group VP of Organization & People Development at Constella Group
Business Growth	Richard Branson	Bill McQuiggan Business development leader at BDM
Thought Leadership	Steve Jobs	Farley Cleghorn Chief Technical Officer at Futures Group
Relationship Management	Winston Churchill Franklin D. Roosevelt	John Cook VP for Health Programs at BDM
Individual Wisdom	Gandalf	Don Holzworth Founder and CEO of Constella Group

As for me, I have been at work on all seven of these dimensions throughout my career. In some competencies, I could teach a course, and in others I still have a lot of work to do. I benchmark myself and my own growth through a combination of measuring against these archetypes and others and particularly my own my internal work, study, and learning toward becoming individually wise.

Hopefully in reading this conclusion chapter of my book, you've come along the journey with me toward becoming a complete leader. If you have read cover to cover, you understand the overall framework and origins for the Complete Business Leader and how each of the seven dimensions fits together into the whole. You will have dived with me into each dimension and gotten a good sense of the key elements, or competencies, of each, as well as specific characteristics of each competency.

Organizational Ethos		
People Leadership	Project Management	Business Management
Business Growth		
Thought Leadership		
Relationship Management		
Individual Wisdom		

Throughout the chapters describing the specific CBL dimensions, I have cross-referenced to other dimensions, conveying the interrelated nature of the seven dimensions. I also highlighted how these dimensions of Complete Business Leadership come to life in the context of an organization and how that organization's specific ethos (mission, core values, operating culture) fundamentally impacts the manifestation of the framework.

In the real-world vignettes I used throughout the book, I have sought to bring these concepts beyond the textbook or academic sphere and into what happens with real leaders on a real journey. In addition to firsthand examples from my own career, I have used examples of real (e.g., John F. Kennedy) and imagined (e.g., Gandalf) leaders and from the domains of politics, military, business, art, and sports. I have, to the best of my knowledge, recorded real-world examples accurately. Hopefully there was enough in there to speak to the listenings of a diverse audience of people interested in leadership.

As I noted in several parts of the book, while the Complete Business Leader framework is conceptual in nature, it has been implemented in practice now at two different companies, Constella Group and Futures Group. At both Constella and Futures, the framework became the primary organizing structure for hiring, developing, and evaluating leaders.

And then after we merged Futures Group with GRM, our GRM colleagues were intrigued by the framework and were interested in its broader application. This is when my friend and colleague Liz Mallas designed and implemented the cohort study of leaders going through specific training around the dimensions of the Complete Business Leader as part of her master's degree program in organizational design.

I have learned much from many along my own journey, experiencing some firsthand and others by observation from afar. I have tried to record these experiences, including quotes or paraphrases, as accurately as possible. If I have mischaracterized an event or individual, I apologize. If I offended someone, I am sorry. I take full responsibility for wherever I have messed up.

I have thought a great deal about whether there is one leader I could point to as the single most Complete Business

Leader who represents the best of *all* of the CBL dimensions. As I noted above, Dwight Eisenhower probably comes the closest.

What I set out in this book as the characteristics of the Complete Business Leader is a pretty high bar. I have highlighted numerous amazing leaders to illustrate specific aspects, and in some cases I have used the same leader in more than one of the seven dimensions. While no leader sets the ideal for every one of the seven CBL dimensions and could thus be called "complete," that doesn't mean we should give up on pursuing completeness. To me, continually working on your leadership craft throughout your life is a high form of professional and life expression.

In the course of the book, I have also attempted to bring some levity to the business of leadership. I think many people (including me) take ourselves so seriously that we need some lightness in the world.

And yet the business of leadership—the results that leadership produces, or not—matters; it's serious work. If we are doing anything at all as leaders, we are causing things to happen that were not just going to happen anyway. Leaders leave an impact. They leave an organization, people, and events hopefully better than they found them. Complete Business Leaders produce meaningful results and cause great things to happen for the world.

You will have heard me describe how leaders see a future and cause that future to become reality. Leaders are all on a journey—every day, really. Some days it is two steps backward and one step forward. Progress is incremental. Other times, progress is dramatic and transformational, as with Eisenhower from 1941 to 1945. Every day and every moment, every small and large thing, every word, every interaction, every decision matters. Eisenhower had been preparing for that transformational time throughout his whole career. The journey of becoming a Complete Business Leader requires a lifelong commitment.

As I noted at the beginning of this book, my intent in writing it was to generously share and make a contribution. Because after thirty-plus years of my own journey, I think I have something of value to share, something that would benefit someone or some noble organizational endeavor, even if in only a small way.

On my own journey, I have had rare and amazing opportunity. Most of it I have seized, some of it not. I have tasted a lot of different memorable "food" along the way. My own wish is to have no regrets, to leave it all out on the field, as they say in sport.

I am deeply grateful to all of those who have shaped and continue to shape me in who I am becoming. And for all readers of this book, I wish you success in your own journey toward becoming complete—a journey that is never finished but is worth taking anyway.

The fun is in the winning. The joy is in the journey.
—Dabo Swinney, head coach, Clemson University football team

Appendix $\boxed{01}$

CBL COMPETENCIES

In the tables below, I summarize the key competencies for each dimension of the Complete Business Leader framework. Within each competency, I list specific outward characteristics or behaviors that, when exhibited, demonstrate the competency. My hypothesis is that each competency can be developed through study and practice; in other words, they are learned behaviors.

These tables shown below are also in each associated chapter, but I have presented them all together here for ease of study and comparison across all seven dimensions.

INDIVIDUAL WISDOM

SUMMARY:
Be a highly effective and self-aware/actualized professional.

KEY LEADERSHIP COMPETENCIES REQUIRED:

Competency	Example Behavior
Curiosity	o Exhibits interest and openness to reexamining previously held beliefs and views o Asks lots of questions
Continuous learning	o Is driven to continually develop, grow, and improve o Reads and studies constantly o Actively seeks out new knowledge
Self-confidence	o Is willing to be vulnerable o Doesn't make excuses and takes responsibility for mistakes o Creates solutions rather than being a victim of circumstances
Courageous	o Displays courage in making hard decisions, having hard conversations, and taking on hard tasks o Goes to the source to solve problems o Acts in spite of fears
Cool under pressure	o Handles ambiguity and uncertainty well o Exhibits calm, clear thinking in the face of chaos or adversity
Independently responsible	o Takes on being the source of what happens o Self-empowers by choosing paths rather than waiting for them to be chosen
Organized	o Prioritizes time, people, and financial resources o Defines what is important and what is not important
Generous	o Invests time freely in individuals and institutions, giving back to others who need it o Freely shares wisdom, insights, and experiences to help others achieve o Nurtures and contributes to others' ideas and initiatives without need for credit

RELATIONSHIP MANAGEMENT

SUMMARY:

Create long-term relationships that result in trust and mutual respect.

KEY LEADERSHIP COMPETENCIES REQUIRED:

Competency	Example Behavior
Institutional representation	o Represents the organization and its values, serving as an ambassador for the organization o Identifies and understands individual and institutional needs and concerns
Taking the long view	o Builds connections with no expectation of immediate return
Building common ground	o Expands and invents possibilities o Seeks mutually beneficial solutions and gains agreement, including scope, budgets, and responsibilities
Mutual respect	o Sets and continually reaffirms mutual expectations o Respectfully pushes back on unreasonable requests and finds ways forward for both parties o Delivers bad news early but with a corrective action plan
Engagement	o Presents ideas and advice clearly o Actively and regularly engages in dialogue o Serves as a problem solver and solution provider
Responsiveness	o Documents client/partner interactions o Is highly responsive via email, calls, and other communications
Standing for the other	o Genuinely seeks the best for another person o Sacrifices self for the interest of others

THOUGHT LEADERSHIP

SUMMARY:

Be a recognized and sought-after expert in your professional field.

KEY LEADERSHIP COMPETENCIES REQUIRED:

Competency	Example Behavior
Active externally	o Proactively and consistently publishes o Is recognized by peers and called upon frequently as a speaker/presenter and advisor o Serves in leadership in professional societies, committees, and workgroups o Is external to the company—excites the market and professional community
Innovator	o Generates "new" and "needed" approaches, methodologies, and tools o Creates and promulgates innovative solution design and problem-solving that advances the field o Offers inputs that carry the weight of evidence o Sees and leverages linkages across disciplines
Active internally	o Serves as a mentor to other professional staff o Is a magnet for attracting professional talent o Inspires colleagues o Is able and willing to help others promote and publish ideas

BUSINESS GROWTH

SUMMARY:

Develop and expand the business.

KEY LEADERSHIP COMPETENCIES REQUIRED:

Competency	Example Behavior
Opportunity development	o Creates opportunities through conversations with clients and partners
	o Creates innovative solutions to solve clients' problems
	o Communicates effectively orally or in writing
	o Identifies new or expanded business opportunities
	o Meets regularly with clients, prospective clients, and partners
	o Qualifies opportunities through research, conversation, and follow-up
	o Exhibits persistence and is not easily stopped
	o Is disciplined in follow-up
	o Understands our value proposition and offerings
	o Understands the marketplace and procurement practices of clients
	o Conveys credibility with clients

Capture management	o Ensures organization is optimally positioned to win a specific new business opportunity
	o Creates distinctions and articulates differentiations with competition
	o Creates innovative, compelling solutions that leverage our offerings and organizational strengths
	o Able to synthesize multiple ideas, disciplines, and stakeholders
	o Creates compelling teaming strategies that offer a differentiated solution for the opportunity
	o Develops and executes capture strategy
	o Drives pricing strategy and ensures technical and pricing strategy are consistent and mutually supportive
	o Negotiates successful arrangements with partners that create a winning team
	o Communicates effectively both internally and externally
	o Makes good decisions about pursuing, bidding, and winning new opportunity
	o Supports communication and team cohesiveness in proposal team
Proposal development	o Integrates understanding, technical approach, management approaches, personnel, and corporate experience into a cohesive, compelling story
	o Prepares effective storyboards and translates into effective proposal text
	o Able to articulate feature/benefits pairs of our proposal approaches
	o Thrives in high-intensity, deadline-driven environment
	o Skilled in defining and communicating proposal win themes and discriminators
	o Skilled in conveying concepts in both graphics and prose

PEOPLE LEADERSHIP

SUMMARY:

Optimize the value of the organization's human capital and cause people to succeed.

KEY LEADERSHIP COMPETENCIES REQUIRED:

Competency	Example Behavior
Selection	o Recruits and hires talented people who fit the organization's needs and values o Builds effective teams
Development	o Provides praise and critique of employee performance o Inspires employees to achieve more than they thought they could o Develops and mentors people to grow professionally o Provides frequent, honest coaching and feedback o Has difficult conversations with employees while ensuring they feel heard and respected
Delegation	o Articulates clear responsibilities, expected outcomes, and accountabilities o Delegates effectively, empowering people while holding them accountable o Sets high but realistic standards and expectations of staff
Example	o Is action and results oriented o Follows company employee performance management systems and processes o Is an effective time manager o Demonstrates company values, code of conduct, and effective management

PROJECT MANAGEMENT

SUMMARY:

Implement projects on time, within budget, and with high quality.

KEY LEADERSHIP COMPETENCIES REQUIRED:

Competency	Example Behavior
Organized	o Understands and optimizes the interrelationships among schedule, cost, and quality o Effective at breaking down work into manageable, trackable elements o Is detail oriented and rigorous in tracking and organizing o Maintains project management documentation that would withstand audit o Optimizes allocation of human resources to project activities to accomplish the project
Disciplined	o Understands and can produce PERT and Gantt representations of schedules o Has working knowledge of MS Project or other project management tools o Is formally trained or certified in project management o Knowledgeable of concepts of earned value management o Has working knowledge of project cost accounting
Analytical	o Can see the big picture and grasp complexity and interdependencies of tasks, people, and processes o Shows ability to predict, assess, and mitigate risks to project performance
Communication	o Exceptional acumen in communicating in all forms to multiple types of audiences o Keeps all stakeholders up to date

BUSINESS MANAGEMENT

SUMMARY:

Contribute to the success of the business enterprise.

KEY LEADERSHIP COMPETENCIES REQUIRED:

Competency	Example Behavior
Governance and legal awareness	o Has knowledge of relevant regulations o Has a working knowledge of legal/contractual agreements and documents o Understands and applies good governance and company policies o Knows when to seek expert legal advice
Risk management	o Understands different contract types and their relationship to company and project-level risk o Understands company business processes and roles and when and to whom to raise issues o Understands and weighs risk/reward tradeoffs
Financial acumen	o Understands relationship between project financials and corporate financials o Understands concepts of sound accounting processes including separation of duties o Understands overheads and their application o Reads and understands income statement, balance sheet, and cash flow statements o Understands the relationship of project costs, revenue recognition, billing, and collections
Strategic perspective	o Understands and applies the organization's business model o Articulates our corporate strategy and how their work maps to the strategy o Makes sound, holistic business decisions, weighing all factors including corporate risk, client relationship, project performance, and people issues and impacts o "Sees" multidimensionally

Appendix $\boxed{02}$

RESOURCES AND TOOLS

Here I have also provided a single table of resources and tools I have found helpful to me as I have studied, learned, practiced, and documented the dimensions of the Complete Business Leader. This table is by no means a comprehensive listing of everything you would need to study or reference to become a Complete Business Leader, but these are some of the most compelling resources and tools I have found. You may have your own to add.

Dimension	Resources and Tools
Individual Wisdom	o *Clear Leadership*, Gervase R. Bushe o *Primal Leadership*, Daniel Goleman o *Authentic Leadership*, Bill George o *The Art of Possibility,* Rosamund Stone Zander and Benjamin Zander o *Crossing the Unknown Sea: Work as a Pilgrimage of Identity*, David Whyte o *Fierce Conversations,* Susan Scott o *The Last Lecture,* Randy Pausch
Relationship Management	o *Getting to Yes*, Roger Fisher and William Ury o *Franklin and Winston: An Intimate Portrait of an Epic Friendship*, Jon Meacham
Thought Leadership	o I don't have any specific outside tools or resources to recommend in the area of thought leadership. What I have learned and described in thought leadership has been experiential.
Business Growth	o www.shipleywins.com o Capturing New Business course (Shipley) o POWeRful Proposal Writing course (Shipley) o Pricing to Win course (Shipley) o *Buck Up, Suck Up . . . and Come Back When You Foul Up*, James Carville and Paul Begala o *Business Stripped Bare: Adventures of a Global Entrepreneur,* Richard Branson
People Leadership	o *The Five Dysfunctions of a Team,* Patrick Lencioni o *X-Teams*, Deborah Ancona and Henrik Bresman o *Building Effective Teams,* Duke Corporate Education o *Servant Leadership,* Robert K. Greenleaf
Project Management	o *A Guide to the PMBOK, 5th edition* (www.pmi.org or other online bookstores)
Business Management	o *The 12-Hour MBA Program*, Milo Sobel o *Strategy for the Corporate Level*, Andrew Campbell, Jo Whitehead, Marcus Alexander, and Michael Goold

General leadership resources	o ***Good to Great***, Jim Collins
	o ***Good to Great and the Social Sectors***, Jim Collins
	o ***Built to Last,*** Jim Collins
	o ***Execution***, Larry Bossidy and Ram Charam
	o ***Exponential Organizations,*** Salim Ismail, Michael Malone, and Yuri van Geest

Appendix 03

REAL LEADERS REFERENCED IN THE BOOK (NOT HOUSEHOLD NAMES)

This table below highlights the names of real people I reference in the book. Each of these had a profound impact on my own learning and leadership journey. In the table, I map the person to the Complete Business Leader dimension where I highlighted them in the book.

Highlighting someone in one dimension versus another does not mean that the person had strengths only in that particular dimension; rather, the table simply serves as a mapping index of one or more dimensions where I chose to highlight a specific leadership example with that person.

NAME	ROLE WHERE I KNEW THEM	CBL DIMENSION	BACKGROUND
Frank O'Brien	My first boss, friend, and mentor	People Leadership Business Growth	Retired Army lieutenant colonel, served as a program director at BDM
David Walker	CFO of BDM and my boss during my finance years	People Leadership Thought Leadership	Well-regarded CFO in the federal contracting market (retired)
John Cook	My boss in the health practice at BDM	Relationship Management Business Management	Retired Air Force lieutenant colonel, focused on health and medical systems
Don Holzworth	Founder and CEO of Constella Group	Individual Wisdom People Leadership Relationship Management	Successful entrepreneur, board member, mentor, lifetime focus on health and well-being
Jane Smith	My executive coach for twelve years	Individual Wisdom	Executive coach with Dorrier Underwood Consulting, writer
Rich Podurgal	VP of Organization & People Development at Constella Group	Thought Leadership People Leadership Individual Wisdom	Former global head of leadership development at GlaxoSmithKline
Rich Cohn	Colleague and friend at Constella Group	Thought Leadership People Leadership Business Growth Project Management	PhD statistician, leading expert on environmental health research

Alonzo Fulgham	Board member at Futures Group, longtime colleague and friend	Relationship Management Business Management	Career member of the senior foreign service, former acting administrator of USAID, serves on multiple boards in industry-leading roles
Farley Cleghorn	Chief Technical Officer at Futures Group and friend	Thought Leadership	Physician and world-renowned leader in HIV research and program implementation
Ron Fitzmartin	External colleague in pharma data management	Thought Leadership	International expert in clinical data management
John Stover	Early Futures Group leader and business colleague	Thought Leadership	World-renowned for family planning and HIV modeling and forecasting
Jesse Milan Jr.	Colleague and friend at Constella Group	Thought Leadership	World renowned leader in HIV advocacy
Bobby Jefferson	Colleague and friend at Futures Group and DAI	Thought Leadership	Leading expert in digital health field
Rodney Wynkoop	Director of the Choral Society of Durham	Thought Leadership	Recognized regional leader in choral conducting
Paul Nedzbala	Colleague at Constella Group	People Leadership	Senior executive leader at General Dynamics IT

Frank Wilkinson	My boss and mentor for a short time in BDM's health practice	Project Management	Expert in IT project management and government contracting management and business development
Shannon Hader	Colleague and friend at Futures Group	People Leadership Business Management	Physician and recognized global health leader; ran CDC's global portfolio for HIV/AIDS, TB, and malaria; recently appointed Deputy Executive Director for UNAIDS
Jim Boomgard	CEO of DAI	Thought Leadership Business Management	International expert on private sector development and micro finance, longtime DAI executive, CEO since 2009

NOTES

1   Online Etymology Dictionary, s.v. "business," accessed May 11, 2019, https://www.etymonline.com/word/business.

2   Jon Meacham, *Franklin and Winston: An Intimate Portrait of an Epic Friendship* (New York: Random House, 2003), chap. 1.

3   Jon Meacham, *Franklin and Winston: An Intimate Portrait of an Epic Friendship* (New York: Random House, 2003), chap. 2.

4   Ken Burns, *The Roosevelts: An Intimate History* (2014), documentary series, episodes 5, 6.

5   Jon Meacham, *Franklin and Winston: An Intimate Portrait of an Epic Friendship* (New York: Random House, 2003), chap. 9.

6   Jon Meacham, *Franklin and Winston: An Intimate Portrait of an Epic Friendship* (New York: Random House, 2003), chap. 1.

7   Richard Holmes, *In the Footsteps of Churchill* (New York: Basic Books, 2005), chap. 9.

8   Jon Meacham, *Franklin and Winston: An Intimate Portrait of an Epic Friendship* (New York: Random House, 2003), chap. 2.

9   Jussi M. Hanhimaki, *The United Nations: A Very Short Introduction* (New York: Oxford University Press, 2008), chap. 1.

10   United Nations (website), accessed May 25, 2019, www.un.org/history-of-the-united-nations.

11   I toured the Churchill War Rooms in London in 2015 and among many amazing things I saw the secure phone booth where Churchill and Roosevelt talked. I was struck by how intimate that made the

relationship. See also Imperial War Museums (website), www.iwm. org.uk/visits/churchill-war-rooms.

12 Richard Holmes, *In the Footsteps of Churchill* (New York: Basic Books, 2005), chap. 9.

13 Jean Edward Smith, *Eisenhower in War and Peace* (New York: Random House, 2012), chap. 12.

14 Virgin Group (website), accessed May 25, 2019, www.virgin.com/ richard-branson.

15 National Archives (website), accessed May 25, 2019, www.eisenhower. archives.gov/research.

16 George Colburn, *The Eisenhower Legacy: Supreme Commander 1941–1945* (2007), documentary.

17 Sara R. Sandock, "Digging Deeper," *PM Network* 22, no. 2, (2008): 70–73.

18 Jean Edward Smith, *Eisenhower in War and Peace* (New York: Random House, 2012), chap. 13.

19 Jean Edward Smith, *Eisenhower in War and Peace* (New York: Random House, 2012), chap. 13.

20 National Archives (website), accessed May 25, 2019 www.eisenhower. archives.gov/research.

21 Robert S. Kaplan and David P. Norton, *The Balanced Scorecard: Translating Strategy into Action* (Boston: Harvard Business Review Press, 1996). The Balanced Scorecard Methodology, developed by Robert Kaplan and David Norton originally in the mid-1990s and documented in their groundbreaking book, became one of the world's best-known approaches to strategic planning and alignment for organizations. It centered around balancing strategies and associated performance measures for coequal perspectives of business planning and management: financial, customer, internal, and learning and growth. The methodology then helps organizations link these four strategic perspectives to tactical execution and measurement. The methodology shifted the thinking of whole industries from focusing solely on financial metrics to other critical aspects of business success.

22 Robert S. Kaplan and David P. Norton, *The Balanced Scorecard: Translating Strategy into Action* (Boston: Harvard Business Review Press, 1996). The Balanced Scorecard Methodology, developed by

Robert Kaplan and David Norton originally in the mid-1990s and documented in their groundbreaking book, became one of the world's best-known approaches to strategic planning and alignment for organizations. It centered around balancing strategies and associated performance measures for coequal perspectives of business planning and management: financial, customer, internal, and learning and growth. The methodology then helps organizations link these four strategic perspectives to tactical execution and measurement. The methodology shifted the thinking of whole industries from focusing solely on financial metrics to other critical aspects of business success.

23 A tool used to give feedback to an employee from their supervisors, peers, direct reports, and others that provides an 360-degree perspective of their performance.

24 Ellen Van Velsor, Cynthia D. McCauley, and Marian N. Ruderman, *The Center for Creative Leadership Handbook of Leadership Development, Third Edition* (San Francisco: Jossey-Bass, 2010).

25 D. V. Day, "Leadership Development: A Review in Context," *The Leadership Quarterly* 11, no. 4, (2001): 581–613.

26 D. V. Day, "Leadership Development: A Review in Context," *The Leadership Quarterly* 11, no. 4, (2001): 581–613.

27 D. L. Kirkpatrick, "Techniques for evaluating training programs," *Journal of American Society of Training Directors* 11, (1959): 1–13; D. L. Kirkpatrick, *Evaluating training programs: the four levels* (San Francisco: Berrett-Koehler, 1994).

28 National Archives (website), accessed May 25, 2019, www.eisenhower. archives.gov/chronologies.

29 Jean Edward Smith, *Eisenhower in War and Peace* (New York: Random House, 2012), chap. 19.

30 Jean Edward Smith, *Eisenhower in War and Peace* (New York: Random House, 2012), chap. 19.

31 Jean Edward Smith, *Eisenhower in War and Peace* (New York: Random House, 2012), chap. 19.

32 Jean Edward Smith, *Eisenhower in War and Peace* (New York: Random House, 2012), chap. 19.

BIBLIOGRAPHY

Burns, Ken. *The Roosevelts: An Intimate History* documentary series, 2014.

Colburn, George. *The Eisenhower Legacy: Supreme Commander 1941–1945* documentary, 2007.

Collins, Jim. *Built to Last*. New York: HarperCollins Publishers Inc., 2002.

Collins, Jim. *Good to Great*. New York: HarperCollins Publishers Inc., 2001.

Day, D. V. "Leadership Development: A Review in Context," *The Leadership Quarterly* 11, no. 4, (2001): 581–613.

Hanhimaki, Jussi M. *The United Nations: A Very Short Introduction*. New York: Oxford University Press, 2008.

Holmes, Richard. *In the Footsteps of Churchill*. New York: Basic Books, 2005.

Imperial War Museums. www.iwm.org.uk/visits/churchill-war-rooms.

Kaplan, Robert S. and David P. Norton, *The Balanced Scorecard: Translating Strategy into Action*. Boston: Harvard Business Review Press, 1996.

Kirkpatrick, D. L. "Techniques for evaluating training programs," *Journal of American Society of Training Directors* 11, (1959): 1–13.

Kirkpatrick, D. L. *Evaluating training programs: the four levels.* San Francisco: Berrett-Koehler, 1994.

Meacham, Jon. *Franklin and Winston: An Intimate Portrait of an Epic Friendship.* New York: Random House, 2003.

National Archives. www.eisenhower.archives.gov/.

Sandock, Sara R. "Digging Deeper," *PM Network* 22, no. 2, (2008): 70–73.

Scott, Susan. *Fierce Conversations.* New York: Berkley, 2004.

Smith, Jean Edward. *Eisenhower in War and Peace.* New York: Random House, 2012.

Tolkien, J. R. R. *The Lord of the Rings Volume I: The Fellowship of the Ring.* New York: Ballantine Books, 1974.

Tolkien, J. R. R. *The Lord of the Rings Volume II: The Two Towers.* New York: Ballantine Books, 1974.

Tolkien, J. J. R. *The Lord of the Rings Volume III: The Return of the King.* New York: Ballantine Books, 1974.

United Nations. www.un.org/history-of-the-united-nations.

Van Velsor, Ellen, Cynthia D. McCauley, and Marian N. Ruderman, *The Center for Creative Leadership Handbook of Leadership Development, Third Edition.* San Francisco: Jossey-Bass, 2010.

Virgin Group. www.virgin.com/richard-branson.

ABOUT THE AUTHORS

CHRISTOPHER (CHRIS) A. LEGRAND

Chris LeGrand currently serves as president, DAI Global Health, LLC, a global health development and consulting company.

Chris has more than thirty years of business experience in the public and private sector services industry, twenty-five of which have been in the health sector. He recently served as CEO of Futures Group from 2008 to 2014 and  in 2016 was appointed as the president of DAI Global Health, a newly launched unit of DAI.

Chris is passionate about the possibility of science and technology innovation as a force for good and putting knowledge and tools in the hands of citizens to make their own lives more fulfilling and communities more free and peaceful. He is committed to the study and practice of leadership, including developing and implementing the Complete Business Leader framework.

Chris is known for his authentic, approachable leadership style and for his ability to create transformation at pivotal times in an organization's history. His leadership style has earned him the trust and respect needed from the boardroom to the junior analyst to drive both the organization's mission and profitable business success. He is a systems thinker, synthesizing people, finance, business development, operations, and technical management. In every leadership role, he has produced results by connecting vision to strategy to execution.

In 2008, Chris led a management buyout of Futures Group from its parent company, SRA International. Futures Group was a $100 million global health consulting firm providing strategic consulting and project implementation to governments in developing countries to improve the health and well-being of their citizens. Futures had subsidiaries and business operations in more than thirty-five countries around the world. Under Chris's leadership, the management team reestablished and repositioned the firm; returned the business to profitability; restructured its financing and substantially paid down its debt; established and organically grew its European business; and successfully engineered the merger of Futures with an Australian company in October 2011.

Previously, Chris was president of Constella Health Sciences, a preeminent provider of integrated health consulting solutions to governments, foundations, and the private sector worldwide. Serving in expanding executive roles, Chris was a key leader in Constella's success, growing from a $14 million niche consulting business to a $200 million global health player. During his tenure, Chris led a successful turnaround of Constella's pharmaceutical services business and was actively involved in eight M&A transactions and integrations. He helped complete the highly successful sale of Constella to SRA in August 2007.

Earlier, Chris spent twelve years with BDM International, a highly respected government services company. At BDM, he had expanding roles, including running large-scale programs for various US government health agencies and commercial clients in the life sciences industry.

Chris serves on several outside boards in the for-profit and nonprofit sectors, including currently serving as board chair for IntraHealth International, a leading nonprofit global health organization. He recently served for four years as board chairman of the Triangle Global Health Consortium and on the executive board of the Council of International Development Companies. He is also active on the board of an NGO based in rural Andhra Pradesh, India.

In the community, Chris is active as treasurer in his church and served for three years as board president of the Choral Society of Durham. He has been the recipient of numerous leadership awards, including *Business Leader* magazine's top 100 Business Impact Leaders in the Triangle of North Carolina and top 40-under-40 leaders in the Triangle (many years ago!). He was honored with the Outstanding Service Award by the Drug Information Association in 2007. Chris holds an MS in information management from The George Washington University and a BS in mathematical sciences from Clemson University.

ELIZABETH (LIZ) MALLAS

Liz Mallas authored Chapter 9 of this book. Liz currently serves as director, Government Affairs for Gilead Sciences. Previously she worked with Chris at Futures Group on a range of business and leadership initiatives, including

launching the Complete Business Leader framework within the company. Liz has master's degrees in public administration from Texas A&M University and in organization development from Queens University. Her undergraduate degrees are in journalism and mass communication and public policy analysis from the University of North Carolina at Chapel Hill. At Futures Group, she served in a series of successively broader leadership roles, having started as an intern and learned every aspect of the business. Her roles included serving in overseas posts in Mexico, Swaziland, South Africa, and the United Kingdom, all the while developing herself as a well-rounded, passionate leader of impactful programs and people. She now lives in Charlotte, North Carolina, where she brings that passion to several community-based organizations and ministries.

Made in the USA
Columbia, SC
12 September 2019